Perfect 40!

How to Live Your Best Life and Age with Grace and Wisdom

LANA SHABDEEN

1st edition, March 2023
Paperback ISBN: 979-8-9880211-0-0
Hardcover: 979-8-9880211-2-4
E-book ISBN: 979-8-9880211-1-7

To my family.

I am who I am today because of you.

"

There is a fountain of youth:
It is your mind, your talents, the creativity you bring to your life,
and the lives of the people you love. When you learn to tap this
source, you will truly have defeated age.[1]
—SOPHIA LOREN

[1] Karen Salmonson, "7 aging quotes: inspiring reminders to feel happy about getting older," *www.notsalmon.com* (blog), Access date December 10, 2021,
https://www.notsalmon.com/2018/11/10/aging-quotes-inspiring/.

TABLE OF CONTENTS

ACKNOWLEDGMENTS

Special thanks to my husband, Rim, for being there for me and supporting me throughout this project. Thanks to my sister, Kristina, for your endless encouragement.

To Michael K. Ireland, my editor, thank you for your guidance. And special thanks to you, my readers. I hope this book helps you persevere when obstacles come to your life. For me, this book might never have been completed if I had given up when challenges tried to force me to stop writing. Instead, I persisted and continued to believe in myself and in this book. So, whatever you do, stick with it. Never give up. That is how dreams come true.

—*Lana*

NOTE TO READERS

Dear Reader,

As you read this book, I invite you to use the Journal pages included at the back to write down your reflections. I have included some worksheets for you to keep track of your progress and what else you need to work on as you contemplate your life and move into mindful living. Enjoy!

—*Lana*

CHAPTER ONE

Perfect Forty!

No matter what year it is, what is happening worldwide, or the latest marketing craze, we cannot help getting older. Even though we cannot help getting older, we do not have to get old. For birthdays, some people, actually most people, feel positive about it. The cheer and joy of being older grasp them tight. Meanwhile, the remaining persons see beyond this. Although they may feel the cheer and joy as well, they also open their minds to the negative part. They see birthdays as one's days on earth being numbered. As a matter of fact, this is very true. The older you get, the lesser your days on earth. This is not meant to instill fear in you. Instead, it is to make you see two basic realities: one will get older, and while you get older, your days are numbered. When is then the perfect age to live life because that is one thing we are all searching for? This book is about the perfect age when we turn 40. It is about how we feel about getting older. This is about aging from the thirties to our forties. This book is not about back pain, knee pain, hair loss, or weight gain when we get close to 40. This is about an emotional rollercoaster, all we think and mentally feel at that age.

There is absolutely nothing that can stop time. Nothing can slow down time. Time machines are the only things close to it. But you know what? Time machines do not exist. Well, they do, but only in the fictional world. The only place where time moves at a slower speed would be in space. After all the fiction movies where traveling back in time is possible, you would really think that something like that is possible in today's technologically advanced world. But even if traveling back in time was possible, it would not guarantee that we would go back to how we looked at that particular time; we would still be the same age we are today, not a minute younger. The time machine only helps you travel back to visit your past, not actually change your age. And when you are done visiting the past, it brings you back to reality. In riddling words, age is the only thing that goes up and never comes down.

For some people, 40 is half of their life, and for others, it is the majority of their life. As crazy as it sounds, this is the truth. You don't have to be religious. You can believe in any faith of your choice. But the only thing we can do about this truth is make the best out of whatever is left out there for us. You should prepare for it and live by it, so you don't need to think of the help of a time machine. Religious or not, one day, we will be gone forever.

So why not call it a Perfect 40? This is a perfect age for everything. Think about it. Why would you not call it a Perfect 40? The forties is the time to make those changes, bold moves, and life-changing decisions. You have not made those changes yet. Suppose you have not taken those bold moves; there may be no better time than today. This is the age when your results come out. You are wondering what your results are, right? You know, as a very young adult, you get advice. Chief of them is that you should live your life without regrets. Thus, do as your heart says. You will be asked to take your steps with your future in mind. We all seek happiness, so they will tell you, you will learn that everything you do should be for your immediate and future happiness. One thing about regret is that it is a future effect. You are most likely not going to feel regret immediately. When they say marry who you love, it is because you will need it later in life. If you don't marry out of love but, let's say, necessity, your marriage will be estranged. Even if you feel the effect immediately, it worsens as time goes by. That time may be around your forties. Age 40 is around the time when your life fully reflects how you have lived your younger years. You will be a representation of the decisions and sacrifices you have made, and your fruits begin to show on you. Is 40 the perfect age? I am here to help you figure it out.

Stop and think for a moment before you go on with the book. What makes life perfect for you? What are the things that you find indispensable in your life? Who are the people in your life that you place a high value on? Do you love simplicity, or do you love the complicated parts of your life? Do you like to wake up early in the morning, or do you love to sleep in? Do you enjoy fresh food, or do you enjoy junk food? Do you enjoy cooking or cleaning? Do you love working out, or are you happy with your random exercise routine? Do you still love partying till late at night or being in bed at 9 in your pajamas and reading a book or a movie? What do you love the most about your day? What do you love the most about yourself?

At 40, you already know the answers to these questions. It is the age where you can confide in your maturity, knowing your choices and decisions are validly informed by the situations you have been through and the circumstances that have been surrounding your life. You are certain as to the events happening in your life. The doubts you had in your early to mid-twenties are gone. You will have learned from your bold mistakes in your 30s because you wanted to take a chance. You will know for sure what makes you happy and what drags you down, and if you do not know, who says it's late to find out? It is a common saying that it is not late until it is late. Until your last breath, self-discovery goes on. If you know that at 40, you are not certain about your life; what you want, what you are, what you love, what you do not like, etc., sit down and write that list. The first thing is to acknowledge that you need to be aware of these things. Self-awareness is fundamental to all humans, and mind you, no one is to make you feel like a failure for not knowing early (40 is not late, ha-ha. It is just 20x2). What's important is that you know it. Get answers to these questions, ask yourself more, think more, and always have your future happiness and well-being in mind as well. 40 is not a late age to start a life at all. Once you write it, eliminate and/or change whatever does not make you happy. Life is too short to waste time on sad, disappointing, dragging, and annoying people and things. At this age, we should not do things to make others happy. We should do things that make us happy. Instead, you should be living off the investments you have made in yourself. The truth is you cannot please everyone, and your happiness is actually yours to make. Others can make the change, and so can you. Do it!

Until we are 40, we do crazy things. We test our limits. We find out what matters to us (and what does not), what political party we like (or if we like a political party at all), which friends go with our flow and just want to binge on Netflix and chill with us (and what friends to avoid), what takeout places we like (and which ones our stomachs cannot handle the next day), what shows we like and dislike, what people make us laugh, what people put us down. The list goes on and on. We know who we are and what everything around us means. We have learned how to overcome challenges and manage our fears. We know what inspires us and what scares us. But at 40, we are just starting to have real fun.

> "
> *Life really does begin at forty.*
> *Up until then, you are just doing research.* [2]
> —CARL G. JUNG

Jung could not have said it better. By the time we reach 40, we have done a lot of research about who we really are. It sounds funny that we did a lot of crazy things before forty, but can the result be compared to the preparation? See it this way. You were preparing for life before 40; you were actually. We are no longer told (or we should not be told) what to do. We have our values, views, and opinions. Throughout the research years, we have let many fears go—or we have learned to live with them. By 40, we have experienced love, hatred, anger, fear, horror, joy, surprise, sadness, betrayal, disappointments, confusion, and jealousy. We have had it all. We had figured out how to handle each and every situation on our own. It is at this age you can tell explicit differences. You will know when you are being played or when you are being abused, or when you are being loved because you have undergone years of varying

---

[2] Carl Jung, www.goodreads.com, Access date December 5, 2021,
http://www.goodreads.com/quotes/4483092-life-really-does-begin-at-forty-up-until-then-you.

experiences. If we had to write a resume about our life for our 40th birthday, we could easily say we are pretty well experienced. Everyone's competency level would obviously be different, but I think just like Microsoft Word, we all have worked with it.

When I turned 39, I had a fear! And I am sure I am not alone when I say the scariest part of life for a lot of women is getting older. There is even a name for fear of getting old— Gerascophobia. It is a form of anxiety or phobia that kicks in and makes us feel like we will never be the same. I know some women do not care about the aging process and just peacefully living the acceptance of the most natural process in life. But this acceptance was not that easy for some of us, including me. That fear is real. I can personally confirm it.

FORTY is that half-life milestone when we transition to being mature women. We say things like, "Oh, I'm getting old." And it is true, we are. After we turn 35, most women are concerned about getting old. Everyone talks about changes that will happen when we get older, but the truth of what that really means does not sink in until we are close to 40! By that time, fear sneaks in—we are afraid of losing our youthfulness, afraid of getting wrinkles, afraid of not having any more kids, afraid of not having enough energy, afraid of having health issues, and afraid that we have not accomplished enough in life.

At 40, some women are still single and have not found their "other half," some have not had kids, and some have gone through a divorce. Others are battling something in their life, have not found themselves, or do not know yet what they want out of life. All these unaccomplished presets in life lead to fears of never completing, never achieving, just never getting it done, and that it is too late. These are all mid-life fears. Some of us experience them at 40, others a little before or after 40. It is very normal to be afraid. It is very normal to feel these fears. But do not validate the fears by accepting their fears. Define yourself and your life by renewing your mind. You must know that 40 is not the end of life, nor is it the end of yours. If not, you won't be reading this book. Instead of settling with your fears, face them. Are you scared of losing your youthfulness? So what? If you lost your youthfulness – the boys chasing you, the outings, and the adventures – is youthfulness all there is to your life? Think about it, is being youthful what determines you, or is it merely a part of you? We are constantly growing, and it is very contradictory to expect our age not to grow with us. As the youthful young age has its peculiarities, so does being 40.

At some point after we pass the 35-year mark, we reflect on who we are, what our purpose in life is, what our values are, who our friends are, and what job we have (and whether we are happy with it). We decide what is important to us. Does this or that thing make us happy or sad? Do we love or hate our job? Do we love or hate the place we are at? Does it bring value to our life? Is it worth our time? There were a lot of questions around that time. Then, depending on what our answers are, we can decide what to do about it. Whatever is necessary, we make changes. If it makes us happy, we should continue. If it does not make us happy or does not bring value to our life, then we need to let it go. And no need to waste our time or wait it out and give it enough time to make it work. None of us knows how long we have on this earth. The 40 mark is a good time to think about life and re-evaluate our time and where it goes, so we do not waste it. This is not only common in women but quite common in men as well. That is when everyone talks about a man having a mid-life crisis. Men go through their midlife crisis by experiencing some of the following: drop in life satisfaction, increased sadness, increased mood changes, spontaneous decision making, a focus on change, ending plans or giving up, frustration and irritability with work, family, or self, and becoming withdrawn.

Once we get close to our 40th birthday, we feel differently about it than we felt about any other birthday we have had. In my instance, I felt scared, worried, and uncomfortable—my biggest fear was that there was not enough time to do everything I wanted. There was so much more to life for me. I wanted to do so much more.

I mean, I have aunties and uncles that were once 40. I remember when they were about that age. And the first thing that came into my head was, 'Do I look as old as they did at 40?' I mean, they looked old (to me, anyway). They looked like they did not care about what they had accomplished in their 40 years of life. It seemed like they did not even care what they wanted to do with the rest of their lives. It felt like they had stopped all their trying and doing just because they had turned 40. They had their spouse; a kid or two—and that was their life. They hated but worked at their jobs. They got an education but did not care for it anymore. They did not pursue their hobbies. They seemed to have stopped growing as individuals. I did not want to be like that. I did not want to feel like that. Even after 50 or 60, I want to continue learning more about life, the world, and new things out there. I want to continue and grow as a person. I want to continue and evolve to be a bigger and better person by learning and exploring. Why stop being someone you want to be after you turn a certain age? Why stop learning and evolving just because of your age?

So, despite all of this, why do I call our fourth decade of life a "Perfect 40?" it is a Perfect age not to care what others think, do what you want to do and not what others are telling you, become whomever you want to become. 40 is a perfect age to become happy, confident, and content and whomever you want to be. Imagine a 40-year-old in your mind. What comes to your mind first is that the person is an adult. And that is the truth. No one gets to shout at you for your decisions. No one gets to direct you on how to live your life. As a matter of fact, people under your age look up to you. It is the age when you have arrived from a long-distance journey. You have been commended and condemned. You have been criticized and celebrated. There is no way at 40. You have not had a vast life experience. Even before this age, some people have experienced more than you can imagine. This is not to say 40 is when you would have experienced all there is in life. You would have discovered the very basic things that will determine a perfect living for you at 40. In simple terms, age 40 is when you would have made a large discovery on matters concerning your life. The number of kids to have, sometimes, the person to spend the rest of your life with, the things you derive great pleasure from. This is it: 40 is that age where you exude an intentional life based on the knowledge you have amassed before 40. This is the perfect age to become the Perfect you at Perfect 40. Hopefully, we have many years ahead of us. We know what we want, or we can just figure it out. The best years are just ahead of us. All our insecurities are behind us. We have learned a lot of lessons and are ready to take on the world. We are ready to live our lives with love and purpose—bravely, boldly, and brilliantly!

Although perfect is an illusion, what word best describes a life that is intentional and determined? You barely have no limitations, your youthful fears are in handy, and you are just so certain about yourself; this is perfect! It is the point where you give out the rules of your life. Perfect may be an illusion, but it has a meaning.

What can you take from this chapter?

It is okay to feel different when your birthday comes. A lot of things have changed in the past year. No one should stay the same. You need to continue to change for the better. The older you get, the more confident you get. You know what you want in life.

Journal Notes

_____

_____

_____

_____

_____

_____

_____

_____

_____

_____

_____

_____

_____

Ask yourself...

1. Are you confident in yourself?

   _____

   _____

   _____

   _____

   _____

   _____

2. Do you know what you like, or do you like what others like?

   _____

   _____

   _____

   _____

   _____

   _____

3. Are you afraid of getting older?

   _____

   _____

   _____

   _____

   _____

   _____

CHAPTER TWO

My Story

One hot summer morning in 2018, I woke up as usual and prepared for the day. It was a beautiful Los Angeles day, perfect weather for the beach. I had slept well, and my daughter was on her best behavior. I had an excellent breakfast that my husband made for me. The weather could not be any more perfect. I was well-rested and ready for whatever the day would bring. Everything was wonderful that morning, but I did not feel 100 percent. I wanted to cry … but I could not figure out why. I was sad. I felt incomplete. I was not worried, I had nothing to complain about, but I was unhappy. I had not fought with anyone. No one made me mad. I was not worried. I had nothing to complain about, but I was not happy. Was I not happy with myself? My Life? What was it?

At the time, I was working for my husband's company, which was doing very well. We had close to 50 employees that I was managing. We just sold the Hospice company that we had. I was working on getting my own brand. My daughter was almost two at that time. She loved her daycare and all her friends. My parents, as always, helped us quite a bit with her. We took a few wonderful trips that year. But still, something was not quite right. Something didn't add up in my life, if that makes sense.

Why did I feel this way? Was this the first time I felt this way? The more I thought about it, the more I realized I had felt like this before—there had been several instances in which I had just wanted to cry for "no reason." I remember this feeling. It was not the first or second time. I had it a few times before. Just a week before that day, I felt the same way. I had a wonderful day at the office, everything was great that day, and I picked up my daughter from daycare and went home. But I fought back the tears—I was not happy. I fed my daughter, had dinner with my husband, cleaned up a bit, got ready for the next day, and went up to my room to spend some alone time with my thoughts. I spent the rest of the evening trying to figure out what it was. What made me feel the way I did? What happened? Maybe someone said something to me, and only now is it getting to me, making me sad. I thought and thought and started to write down all the possibilities that could have made me feel the way I did. Nothing really stood out from my list that could have caused such unhappiness within me. I went to sleep, hoping for a better day tomorrow.

Learn from yesterday, live for today, and hope for tomorrow. The important thing is not to stop questioning.[3]
—ALBERT EINSTEIN

For the next few weeks, I felt the same most days. Obviously, that just took me to the next level of thinking. I could not stop thinking about why I felt the way I felt. I spent some time alone again and again and took long drives before coming home. I went to a park a few times during my lunch break for some fresh air and to be alone. I knew I had to get this figured out some way or the other.

Well, all this thinking, drives, and walks alone helped me figure it out. After digging deeper into my feelings, I simply realized I was unhappy with myself. Not only that, but I also found out that I was also afraid of getting old. I looked at the pictures of me from ten years ago and realized I had looked so young then. My skin looked different. I felt different. My body did not have random aches and pains. I had so much more energy! So many things came to my mind about how I was not

[3] Albert Einstein, www.brainyquotes.com, Access date December 5, 2021, http://www.brainyquote.com/quotes/albert_einstein_125368.

the same youthful, energetic, young-looking woman I had been at twenty-six. I was getting older and older—not younger. What a silly thing to think and say, right? I looked at myself in the mirror. I looked at my body—at the extra pounds I had put on. I was not happy. I was afraid it would be worse. I will have more and deeper wrinkles, more pains in my body, and never be younger again. I was devastated.

So, I started to write things down, dissecting one thing after another. Writing things down always made it easier for me to put things into perspective. Writing things down helps me think things through differently. Writing things down also helps me prioritize, organize, and put goals. I gave it some thought, looked at myself head to toe, wrote down all the things I did not like and the things I liked, and asked myself, "What can I do to make myself feel and look better? What can I do to change the feelings that I have? What can I do to never feel the same way I felt a few times before?"

After some time, I came up with a few action items. I decided I would take better care of myself, focus more on myself, exercise more, eat healthier food, drink collagen, do anti-aging facials, and do all I could to slow down the aging of my skin and body. It was time for Botox, so I went and got that done. I picked out dressier outfits for work, they were different than my usual "uniform," per se, and they made me feel a little better. There I decided I would pick my outfit daily, bad or good mood, but not rush into my "standard outfits" on a daily basis. I decided to eat healthier and good-for-me foods, more soups and salads, more fruits and veggies, and reduce my sugar intake. I would try my best to maintain the best diet possible for me. I promised to do all I could to care for myself and my body. I would do all I can to help my body be healthy, which will help me feel and look healthier in the long run. I didn't want body aches, but I understood exercising was the first thing I had to do, and do it consistently.

Second was the diet, on which I had agreed before. I started to take some classes. Eventually, I hired a personal trainer and worked out twice a week. I signed up for a gym membership, so I could be more active in addition to personal training. Bought more workout clothes and made being active a priority for me. I had to make those changes for myself. I could not expect a result without putting a lot of effort into it. At that point in my life, I just had to do it. I had to do it for me, for my sanity, for my overall well-being, and for my future.

A few months into my work on myself, I started to notice I started to get compliments from people around me. Honestly, and maybe obviously, it made me feel great. At that point, I began noticing a change in how I felt as well as in how I looked. I was motivated even more! I made sure I was as consistent as I could be. I tried harder; things started to get easier. I did all I could to a certain extent. I put my 100% into it, knowing that if I do not do it, no one else will do it for me. I knew I was doing something right, and as I felt better, I felt a change in me overall.

While I was focusing on myself, I also realized how much more I got to see and learn. I started to look at things from a different perspective. I started to see people differently. I started to realize what actually mattered to me the most. Once I started the change, the rest of the good changes just followed on their own. I loved it as it allowed me to grow more and more as an individual.

A few years passed, and I turned 39. I realized, "My next birthday is the big 4-0! Holy cow!" I could not believe it. And after my 40s, that's four decades ... the next decade is 50! I did not feel that way when I turned 30. I was not worried to be turning 40 when I turned 30! When I turned 30, I don't think I even thought, 'where did my 20s go?'. Why now? What was such a big deal? At this point, I was really taking care of myself. But how I felt about turning 39 was so odd, so different, so disorienting. I thought I was that aunty! The one I remember had no ambition, no desire to take care of herself, and no goals in life. Even though that aunty is from the 1990s, but still made me think. Do I look like I remember my relatives looking? Do I act like I remember them acting? Do I dress like the aunty I remember? Do I have goals? What are my goals outside of the family? Am I still ambitious? All these questions and more went through my mind.

Once again, I took my favorite pen and paper and started to write things down. I wrote down my short-term and long-term goals, what I liked, and what I still wanted to change in myself. What would make me feel comfortable in my shoes? At this point, I could care less what another person thought about my actions, my words, and whatever else they decided to discuss. I wanted to focus on ME, what I wanted. In addition, I was scared. Lots of different things were running through my head that day. I had never felt so emotional about turning a year older. So that day, April 1, 2021, I went for a walk, thinking, "What now? What do I do? I cannot stop getting older. I cannot reverse aging. I have been down this road before." I made some good changes a few years back, but here I was, thinking about my age. With all the technology out there, yes, there are things I can do to change my appearance. Plastic surgery has no limits. But one day, even with plastic surgery, age will show. As much as I want to run away from it, the universe makes the rules, and I have to follow them.

Later as I was reminiscing about aging, I tried to remember if anyone older than me—a little or a lot older—had spoken to me about how they felt regarding turning a certain age. No one ever had. I mean, yes, after a certain point in life, we all say we do not like birthdays, do not talk about our age, do not want to get older, and so forth. But no one ever talked about how awkward it *feels* to turn a year older.

So, I started to look for explanations. I started googling. I was looking for blogs. I was looking for chats. I was looking for any information that could give me that support to tell me it is ok what I am feeling and that I am not alone. I searched and searched and searched, and all I came across was information about menopause, perimenopause, what to expect when you turn 60, and so forth. There were so many other results Google returned —from wrinkles to things to do to look younger to 40 things to do before you turn 40 - the hits went on and on. But there were no answers. Nothing calmed me down. I could have gone to my mom or my older sister, but I did not want to alarm them or have them think, "Lana's going crazy!" As I researched more, I discovered the answer: it is within me. I can find peace, strength, and happiness—it is all about my mindset. Later in the book, I will explain what I discovered and share the details with you.

What can you take from this chapter?

It is okay to feel emotional about getting older. You need to listen to your body and mind. If something bothers you, you need to pay attention and figure it out. You will not just ignore it. You will make the changes you wish to see, even if it is one step at a time.

Journal Notes

_____

_____

_____

_____

_____

_____

_____

_____

_____

_____

_____

_____

_____

_____

Ask yourself...

1. Have I noticed a change in me, physical changes, or mental changes?

_____

_____

_____

_____

_____

_____

2. What changes have I noticed?

_____

_____

_____

_____

_____

_____

3. Am I okay with the changes?

_____

_____

_____

_____

_____

_____

CHAPTER THREE

It's a process
that takes time

After Google didn't turn up a lot of results and I couldn't find any books that I could get my answers from, and since I figured all the answers were within me, I decided that I needed to speak to someone about it from someone I knew, someone I felt comfortable with. I decided to speak to my sister and my mom. I definitely felt comfortable with them in hopes of getting some answers.

So, one day I talked to my sister, Kristina, who is now 45. We are pretty close. She is my best friend, but we never spoke about getting older or how we felt about it. One morning I bluntly asked her, "How did you feel about getting older? Did you think about getting older? Or was every birthday just a regular birthday for you? Did you have any fears associated with getting older? Anything that really worried you that had to do with getting older? Did you experience the same things I did?" I asked. "Did you have the same worries? What changed about your perspective on life with every year? Did you feel any difference between your 30s and 40s?"

As long as I can remember, I had teased Kristina about being four years older than me. I was mean about it, too. I am not proud of that now, but it was fun then. During that conversation that I had with her, I had an opportunity to apologize to her as well, as one only realizes what it feels like once one is in those shoes. So, it was a lengthy conversation.

"I had the same feelings and worries, too," Kristina told me. "But my feelings and worries differed completely from my late 30s. They differed significantly from when I turned 41. Other than the obvious physical changes most of us feel and see, I questioned my inner strengths the most. When I was about to turn 40, I looked at my strengths and weaknesses and realized, 'I cannot be the best at everything, and that's okay.' I looked at myself from different perspectives and realized I was good at some things but not so good at others. I realized we are all unique; there is no single person like me on this earth. I should not compare. I accepted I could be weaker at some things and stronger at others. I realized where I have my pluses, and I acknowledged my value. That helped me see I was not alone. A lot of women feel this way around 40. I understood who I was as a woman. I realized that positive thinking could lift me up and how important it was for me to maintain a higher vibration and sustain positive thinking. Whenever I needed to be uplifted, I tapped back into a high vibration and would feel better in no time! I figured it out, and it worked for me. Everyone has their own way. You should find your way."

This is the hard reality of women. They look at you as you age but don't know if some things are going down with you. Most women have this fear of getting older. This fear is what begets the worries most women have during their forties. This fear is anchored on the perception or belief that life is best at the adolescent age or around the thirties. In the words of the great philosopher Socrates, "an unexamined life is not worth living." To express, in other words, a life that is not predicated on self-discovery and self-awareness is not a life.

Think about your younger days and what we have been saying so far. To a very large extent, a young life is yet unexamined. It is merely undergoing the examination process. But this is not understood by many. We think so much about our younger days and place so much emphasis on the things we did or did not do. We do not, at most times, consider that there is more. You worry about your body size, worry about your skin, worry about your life. All these worries emanate from the so much value we placed on our younger days without or with little consideration for how the older days can be better.

"

Our strengths are our tools, our personal reality.
Our Weaknesses are only what we are not.[4]
—JOSEPH BATTEN

Kristina also explained how important it was for her to find her higher power. A higher power is something like something that keeps you on your positive vibrations. For some, it may be meditation, prayers, simple walks, and listening to mantras, music, or whatever elevates you back to who you want to be. Everyone has it. That higher power eventually turns into inner power. We just need to work on ourselves and figure it out. It takes time, but once you find it, no one and nothing will take you down. If you can pull yourself out of negativity, you are set. If you can put yourself together and lift yourself, nothing can ever keep you down. And if something ever pulls you down, you are sure to get back on your feet. This is some serious inner power that you create by finding your higher powers. We all believe in something, something greater than us. We just need to find that connection.

---

[4] Joseph Batten, www.picturequotes.com, Access date November 26, 2021, http://www.picturequotes.com/our-strengths-are-our-tools-our-personal-reality-our-weaknesses-are-only-what-we-are-not-quote-198452.

I kept telling Kristina how bad I felt for teasing her so much about her being four years older than me and all that she had gone through. Because here I am, four years younger and having the biggest fear of my life – to get older. Talking to Kristina brought me a lot of relief and made me realize I was not alone with my crazy thoughts about who I was and where my life was headed. After the conversation, I dug even deeper into my life to find myself and my answers.

Then the other day, it was perfect timing, and I decided to ask my mom how she felt about getting older. Mom said she only thought just a little about getting older, and it was just recently. Throughout the years, she has been so busy with kids, and grandkids, working, cooking, and cleaning. She didn't really have time to think about getting older. So, I wondered, maybe this subject is different for everyone. Or maybe worrying about getting older is generation specific? Maybe my generation looks at aging differently than my mom's. Perhaps I was the only one really worried about aging? Whatever it was, I just knew I was not alone.

My understanding that I am now in midlife did not take me a day, a week, or a month—it took a few years to realize that my body, skin, mentality, and everything about me is changing. This is something that you don't notice overnight. Even though this change seemed to happen faster than any previous change in my life, it was not the easiest. It took a few years, but a lot happened in a brief period. After everything I had learned over this time, one thing was certain; I wanted to show my two daughters that age is just a number. I wanted to set a good example for them. I wanted to age gracefully and show them it is okay to love yourself at whatever age you are. At first, this seemed like Mission Impossible. I was confused. How could I accept my aging and teach the right thing simultaneously? I had to find a way!

I started to write down all my achievements in my life. I had to dig deep to ensure I did not disvalue any of them, as one was as important as the other. I wrote down all of them, from working full time while graduating with a bachelor's degree to keeping up with my marriage while going to school and working full time, keeping in touch with family without missing any important dates and holidays, giving birth to my daughters and getting through all the wonderful things that come with pregnancy, childbirth and keeping up with having additional responsibilities, all the sleepless nights while working full time and helping my husband run a company. The list went on and on. That list made me feel great! I mean, amazing. I didn't really realize how strong and determined I actually was till about that point.

Then I wrote down all my regrets, all my downfalls, all that I was not happy about that I did, and all my mistakes. I wrote about how I have mistreated some people, how I hurt some close people to me, how I believed some people and didn't trust my heart and accused them of things without asking them first, and how I acted in some instances. This list went on and on, and I was proud to find that I could find them and point them out, as to all honesty finding my mistakes was as important as finding my achievements. From there, I realized I owed some an apology. I apologized, and even though it may not have changed much, it gave me relief that I found a better self and was ready for some sort of change in my life.

Writing those lists really triggered some change. I felt happier, more mature, and more relaxed. I realized that being a certain age means nothing. What matters is when you become wiser, one way or the other, through life experiences and understanding what life is all about. If you don't act as a wise person and if you do not treat others with respect, then do you learn anything at all throughout your life? That seemed to be one of the clues for me to become a happier me.

Then throughout the next few months, every day took time for me to be alone with my thoughts. I was working hard and trying to find more answers, and on my way through this aging process dilemma, I achieved what I needed to achieve. When I actually turned 40, I felt like my life pivoted 180 degrees. I have become more aware of myself and who I am. My confidence has gone through the roof—I did not care about people's opinions anymore; I did what made me happy. I found my inner power, which my higher power has helped me to find. I was set on what and whom I liked and disliked. I have accepted the fact I will continue to age ... with grace! That is why I call this milestone in life a "Perfect Forty."

Instead of asking why this age should be called perfect, ask why age 40 should not be perfect. It is clearly an age of manifestation. You have been led, fed, and so on prior to 40. From 40 is when you show the world what you truly are. Sometimes as young adults, people overlook the things we do or forgive them on the premise that we are young and thus incapable of making firm and wise decisions. But as a full-grown adult, like a 40-year-old adult, people can't give you that privilege. Instead, there is a subconscious expectation in everyone that you should know what you are doing and that you are capable of avoiding flimsy mistakes; that, which they regard as the hallmark of adolescents and young adults. This is the general expectation of people. But deep down, you have your own fears of getting older. You will not blame the people for not seeing through this fear because, after all, we are all humans, incapable of reading through minds,

These fears are valid, but the age of 40 is not one to live in fear. From my encounter with the fear of getting older and my discussions with both my mom and sister, it is explicit that there are processes. There is something popular they say about processes. They say, "give yourself to the process, and you will get the result." In other words, it means you may not get the result of the process if you don't submit to the process. I said that if there is one thing that I have learned from talking with my sister and mom, it is that I am not in this alone. That is not to suppose I derive joy in knowing I am not in this situation alone. Rather, it gives me the impression that I am normal and that this fear of getting older is a natural feeling. I had feared them, but they are no more. I can confidently say that it is because I submitted to the process. That feeling of voidness that is prompted by getting old has been taken care of. The emotional troubles that come with getting older are something you can deal with; I speak from experience.

The process of dealing with your fears of getting old takes time, just like it took time for the fear to develop and be realized. You didn't wake up one day and started feeling afraid of getting old. You didn't wake up over the night and start worrying about the wrinkles on your face believing them to be selling you off as an old woman. You didn't wake up after a night's sleep and started feeling 'old.' As a matter of fact, when these fears loom in, they come under disguise. Immediately, you don't realize what is actually wrong with you. Take my story, for instance. It started with my emotions. The fears messed with my emotions such that even though I had a "good life," I was still not satisfied and happy. There was an emptiness I felt. I only discovered what was wrong after a thorough examination of myself; "an unexamined life is not worth living."

I began active steps towards solving this issue because I just can't live the rest of my life feeling that way; that would drive me totally crazy. Truthfully speaking, it might mess with my mental stability, thus affecting my mental health. And that is not peculiar to my case. It can actually happen to anyone.

Age 40 is obviously when this kind of feeling and other related feelings start to manifest. The good news is that you don't have to feel that way about life. You can always correct things. The first process is to find the cause of the way you feel. You do that by thinking. Give yourself time; you don't have to figure it out in a day. Remember, the process takes time.

You may decide to confide in someone close to you as I did. You can ask questions about getting older and what comes along with it. Search these answers with your happiness in mind. What people should read from your life is not that "being old is really frustrating." People always watch what we do as humans. Even when they don't want to, they look at your life to find some things, to feed their curiosity, and to answer the lingering questions in their mind. If you do nothing about these fears associated with getting older and all you do is try to cope with them, it will reflect. Though people may not interpret it exactly as it is, they won't interpret it well. Conversely, if you deal with these fears, you open the way for yourself to feel more peace and happiness. For instance, you used to maintain a scale of weight in your younger day, but as you're getting older, you seem to be losing it. It starts to make you feel a bit unhappy because you don't like how you appear.

Get into action! What can you do to make your situation better? Find thing(s) to do about the situation, and don't linger in the thoughts of your fears. When you've done something, people will see and think of how an older person is in shape like you are. But more importantly, you will love yourself more. As for me, there is a particular model, around 60 years. I wonder how she cheated nature because she does not look her age at all. Although I know in this age of technological advancements, she may have employed the use of enhancements. However, she made an effort.

I invite every woman reading this book to think about what has happened this far in her life and to look at her achievements, big and small. Look at all the mistakes you have made, all the lessons you have learned, all the tears you have shed. Write them down. Pat yourself on the back. You have made it this far. See if there are any ties you can cut, apologies you can make, and mistakes you can fix. Do it. You will become a better version of yourself. Don't do it for anyone. Do it for yourself. The next level of adulthood is what you are entering. You have come this far—the rest of it is a breeze.

What can you take from this chapter?

Do not stay quiet. You should talk to someone of a similar age. Others are probably feeling the same way you do about the challenges of aging. Remind yourself of all the experiences you have had. Forgive yourself for any mistakes. We all make mistakes. Fix mistakes and apologize if you can. Take time for yourself every day. Take a few hours, one hour, or a few minutes, and reconnect with yourself. You will get a lot of answers.

Journal Notes

_____

_____

_____

_____

_____

_____

_____

_____

_____

_____

_____

_____

Ask yourself...

1. Have you talked to anyone about how you feel?

   _____

   _____

   _____

   _____

2. Would you feel better if you spoke to someone that is close to you in age?

   _____

   _____

   _____

   _____

3. Do you do at least one thing for yourself each day?

   _____

   _____

   _____

   _____

4. Do you appreciate all your experiences and achievements?

   _____

   _____

CHAPTER FOUR

The Number Forty

"Do not worry! Age is just a number on your driver's license." How many times have you heard that encouraging statement? I have heard it more than a hundred times and said it to others more than a hundred times as well. My friends used to say, "So what, Lana? So, you are almost 36 (or 37, or 38, or 39). It is just a number." So true. But when I turned 39, I felt different. "It's only a number" did not sound calming anymore. I did not love being 39. Also, have you heard when an older woman loves or falls in love with a younger man, people say, "age is just a number"? Obviously, they say these things about age to take your mind off the feeling that you are not doing something at the right age. However, there is a truth to that simple statement. Age is actually just a number.

Tell me, aside from the figures that represent the age, what else is there to your age?

I loved turning 30. Everything was certain. Complete. I was set. I knew what I wanted to do (or so I thought). Turning 30 felt like I had stopped being a teenager. I wanted to do things I liked, not what others liked. I was married. I wanted kids in my 30s. Even though being pressured because we were not starting a family was a huge thing. But before that, I wanted to have some more fun and travel. My husband and I were fortunate— we traveled the world and made great friends all over the globe. Then decided to start a family once we were ready and not when others felt we should have started.

Everyone lives their life the way they choose. Some have kids in their 20s, some in their 30s, and some in their 40s. Some decide to focus on their careers. Some decide to travel the world and then settle down in some other parts of the world. But we have a very different mentality when we are in our 20s. But 40 is gold.

Anything before 40 is Life 1.0. Anything after 40 is Life 2.0. It has nothing to do with the numbers; it is more about maturity levels and stages of life. In Life 1.0, we have tried everything (or most of it). On the upside, we want to impress people. We are partying, getting drunk, getting into trouble, getting married, and having a kid or two. On the downside, we are getting divorced because we either rushed into it or were too young and did not see the person we fell in love with for who they really were, getting into trouble with a friend, getting DUIs, and so on.

In Life 2.0, we are doing what we like. We know what we dislike, who we attract, and who attracts us. Let us take the life of a woman, for instance. Her name is Hilary. She's the second of four children in her family and the youngest daughter. As a child, she grew up healthily under her parents. They had issues but not much to make the family an estranged one. Like her older sister, her father likes her also and even more than the boys. She grows into an adolescent and starts experiencing puberty. She crushes on a boy in her class in high school. One guy does not like her the way she does, but another likes her more than she likes her crush; you know, just another of those high school love stories. She tries a lot to get his attention. Makes a lot of impressions. Finally, she gets over the feeling. She picks Literature as her major. She likes to read and wants to write books when she grows up. She goes to college, gets a degree, and starts her life fully. Unlike when she was younger, she no longer gets frequent calls from her father, nor does she receive the occasional calls from her mother. She is free from her monitoring sister and has settled into an apartment of hers. She works so hard so she can afford to stay alone, and she does. Some of the reasons she wants to stay alone are attached to her experiences in college. She did not quite enjoy the company of her roommates. She falls in love more. At some point, she endured a relationship because she was bent on making things work because she is a strong believer in the saying that "people have the power to make anything work." She stays in the relationship for a while until she meets another man, the one she's been in a relationship with now for 11 months. According to her story, he defined love for her. She knew what it meant to be loved by him. Although she knew all this while, he just validated the feeling. She is now 28 and is working on her first book. She has been writing but has never published a book. This first book of hers is like a documentary of her experience. It's a book on relationships. She gets married to her man at 29, and they begin their married life. Hilary is happy in her marriage because she is so sure she chose right, and even though they have issues of theirs, they still get along. She gave birth to three children as she and her husband had agreed. The last child she gave birth to was at age 37. Hilary has had her own version of ups and downs in her life. She meets people from high school and college and compares herself a lot. Hilary finds a way to sort out her issue because she realizes she is at a point in her life where she has dependents who look up to her constantly. She wants to be the best example to them. She spoke with her husband, and he stood with her through the tough times, as he should. On her 40th birthday, Hilary launches the publication of her second book, a novel. She prepared very well for the birthday and looked so gorgeous on that day. Her guests could not help but talk about her from ear to ear. She enjoys the atmosphere of being the subject of all adoration and admiration. Someone, her friend, tells her after the birthday celebration that she overheard some people talking about how they admire Hilary so much because of her accomplishments and her life. Hilary herself could not help but admire herself greatly. She thinks about past times when she had trouble keeping up with people and their expectations. Now that she is doing her life the way she feels best, she feels so peaceful, unlike her college days when she tries to avoid people because of this issue. She thinks about her children, about her career, and commends herself. She thinks about her past and mistakes and says to herself, "that is gone forever. This is me now, and I have learned from them." Basically, Hilary built her life on the experiences she has had right from her immediate family, friends, and family. She figured out what's best for her, and the happy life shoots at 40.

Although this story is tailor-made, it is conjured to fit into the subject of this chapter, but this can as well for a person's real story. I am also sure that even though you cannot relate entirely, you can relate to Hilary's life to an extent. People usually dismiss it as a myth that life begins at 40, but if we do the math, life actually begins in this fourth decade. This is the average age when people begin to enjoy or benefit from their carrier. It is unarguable that in marriages, children are regarded as gifts, and no parents don't love their children. Many people see their children as achievements. It is around the age of 40 that achievement is mostly achieved. The largest hallmark of the fourth decade is the level of confidence. At this age, you have built up a level of confidence that can easily resist the whims of people. Another is the certainty that comes with your decisions and actions. At most times, you are very sure as to what to do and what decision leads to your happiness. You are a commander of your life and probably some lives, too, if you've got them.

We may still be confused about a few things, but we are ahead of the game compared to where we were on our 30th birthday. Being confused is a good thing because that means we think we have options. Confusion is a roadblock, and those are wonderful as it forces you to find another route. In Life 1.0, we rushed into decisions, and we took a lot of chances. And eventually, we pay for all of our decisions and chances in Life 2.0.

Since 40 is only a number in Life 2.0, we can still do everything we want to do in our life. We just need to make sure our thoughts and others' opinions do not block us. Filtering your surroundings and choosing the people you socialize with is particularly important. If friends, family, or colleagues tell you, "You are old. You cannot (or should not) do whatever you want (whatever it is that you want to do)," you should ask them to be quiet, take a few steps back, or disappear from your life altogether. You do not need negativity in your life! You are still young. If you still want to, you can do all the things you wanted to do when you were 20.

So, what they will come back with "You see, I told you not to do that, you wouldn't like it," "I told you this was not for you," and so on… Some say it because they love you, some say it because they hate, some say it because they just love to judge others, and others will just find something to say just simply because that will make them feel better about their life. So, guess what? Either way, naysayers will judge you. So why would you care?

A woman has the age she deserves.
The age of a woman is not important: you can be wonderful in
your 20s, amazing in your 40s, and stay
fabulous for the rest of your life. [5]
—COCO CHANEL

A lot of my friends who are around 40 still want to run a marathon, get into shape, scuba dive, skydive, climb Kilimanjaro, get a bachelor's degree, have kids, get married, travel the world, find a hobby, get remarried, have more kids— they want to do so much. So, they should! So, what, get your pilot's license, get another degree, change career, travel the world, volunteer? Do whatever it is you have always wanted to

[5] Coco Chanel, www.azquotes.com, Access date December 5, 2021, https://www.azquotes.com/quote/1358434.

do or just decided that you want to do. There is no better time than now!

The other night, my husband and I went out for dinner with some old friends. We met them in our late teens—we have known them for over twenty years! We went to a posh LA restaurant for dinner and drinks. It was great to catch up with them, as we had not seen them since the Pandemic. As we were talking, the question of everyone's age came up. Someone said, "Lana, you've changed little in twenty years—if anything, you've gotten better with time, like a fine wine!"

It is true that I have been taking care of myself, my skin, what I eat, and everything else in the past few years … more than I did before. But I do not think these are the biggest reasons I have "aged like a fine wine." As I have worked with my fears and questions in the past few years, I have realized that the actual number, the age, is just a number, and it does not matter. It is the happiness within me. It shows. I am happy in my life 2.0. I am busy with all the things I love, which is more important than any number.

Age has no limitations. The only limit is what you set for yourself. It's not about a number. It's about your quality of life, the boundaries you set for yourself, your goals, and your purpose in life. You really just pick what you want for yourself. If you want a busy life, if you want a quiet life, if you want to travel or work more. If you want kids, get married, or get divorced, it is really what you want, not what the numbers tell you. This is what your life should be premised on; what you have discovered for yourself that is best and suits your life. Your life should not be dictated by what others think, perceive, or feel. If there is something I have realized in this life, it is that whatever you feed your mindset with is what you will be. Someone once told me this, but I rebuffed it until I saw that it's actually true. That lady told me, "If you believe in something, it will work for you. If you don't believe, it won't work for you." This is not a supernatural thing. It's just a way of how things work with the information in our minds and our reality. It exposes the fact that our reality is an expression of our beliefs. What's the point I'm making? Age 40 is a filtering age. It is that point where you reserve only the information, knowledge, and idea that is healthy for your life. Discard all you have garnered intentionally and unintentionally over the years. 40 is the beginning. You express those lovely, lively, and peaceful thoughts about yourself. If you tell yourself that 40 is not a number and it really matters in your life, that is exactly what your life will reflect. On the flip side, if you tell yourself if you hold the belief that age is just a number, your life will reflect just that. When people see you, they see a woman who they want to be like, whether young or old. But if you are on the former side, what will be of your life is that you will be admiring the life that you yourself have limited yourself to. You must understand that you are your own limitation. No, age doesn't come close. Career-wise, emotionally-wise, relationship-wise, financially-wise, be the woman you want to be, never minding your age. Old women - women aged about 60-70- still attend school to get degrees. There is no way they have not gotten discouragements from people trying to dissuade them from pursuing a degree at their age. Eventually, when we read about them, we think, "oh, what a determined woman!" they did get discouragements, but it didn't define them. Life ought to be just like that: not living by the terms of people but by your informed terms. 40 is selected as the perfect because whatever prior experiences you have had before then is more than enough for you to live by. That is what you should do. Make your life a reflection of your selected choices. People may not agree or like it, but it's whose life?

If you say 40, you want to be a 40-year-old woman. You will be. If you say you want to be a baby girl for life, you want to rock for life, you will. This is exactly what 40 is about; the real you in action and manifestation.

What can you take from this chapter?

Remember, age is just a number. That number has nothing to do with your goals, your dreams, or your achievements. Remind yourself (every day if you must) that age is just a number. Set a reminder on your phone, on a Post-it® note next to your dresser, or somewhere you will see it first thing every morning. Remind yourself whatever you have to remind yourself every morning or every day. Lastly, no one should tell you that you are too old. You can do whatever you want at whatever age you want.

Journal Notes

_____

_____

_____

_____

_____

_____

_____

_____

_____

_____

_____

_____

Ask yourself...

1. Do you let others tell you what you can and cannot do?

    _____

    _____

    _____

2. Do you take care of yourself honestly and fairly?

    _____

    _____

    _____

3. Is there anything you wished you did more of? If yes, what?

    _____

    _____

    _____

4. Create a plan of action. Start with one thing—and once that is a habit, add another thing. Do not pile them all up at once. If you have not done it yet, you will not do everything all at once now.

    _____

    _____

    _____

CHAPTER FIVE

The
inappropriate talk...

I have heard that it is inappropriate to ask a woman her age. A large number of people share that opinion, generally. Whether a man or a woman, they feel it is inappropriate to ask for a person's age. Some people pop the question in the middle of conversations, and some, are outside conversations. Some ask about meeting you, and others ask after meeting you. Whenever the question is being asked, it is because the one who asks wants to base a conclusion on the answer. Or rather, they may have made a conclusion but still want to justify it with your instance. For instance, a young girl of 12 years is very smart and answers some critical questions. Then someone wonders how this very young girl is able to do that. "She must be older than she looks," the person would say. Then she asks the girl, and she says, "I'm 16 years." "I said it!" or, it could be that the person had not considered her to be an older girl with a younger face. So instead, he thinks, "She's very smart for her age." "How old are you?" he asks to clear the air of ambiguity.

Not only are adults being asked the age question, but children are also being asked as well. However, asking children is not considered inappropriate. As for adults, the question is being asked for various reasons. Let's say a man meets a woman. They start to talk, and he asks the question. In this instance, he is most likely asking to know if they are compatible for a relationship (because the predominant practice is that men are always older in relationships. Some consider that way the best combination. Others don't mind; age is just a number). When someone meets an unmarried woman, who is obviously not in her twenties and asks the age questions, it is most likely to determine how long she has been single.

Generally, people attach an age to success. So, when they see a young person who is very successful in their ventures, they say, "he/she made it early. She's so young." The perception of life is that as people grow older, they become more successful. So, when they see a young-looking person that is very successful, the thinking is that he has achieved beyond his/her age. On the flip side, when they see an older person with little success (in their opinion), they think he/she is behind in life. That is generally regarded as a failure by some. When they hear a woman is 38 and unmarried, people consider her a failure because, at that age, it is expected that you should have married at least and have kids. Some women even use it against themselves. A simple conflict may arise between two women, married and unmarried, and the married one will easily rub her marriage on the other's face because, at least to her, she has achieved something. Age is the parameter for success, but that is not what it ought to be.

You must have heard that "variety is the spice of life." There are different individual meanings that can be ascribed to that saying. The most obvious meaning of that saying is that humans are different, and a direct implication of that is there will be differences in all we do. Although similarities may exist, the core thing is that no person is another person. Even twin children are not the same person. As they are different persons, they have different stories, names, ambitions, happiness, mindset, and success. Yes, they may both have the ambition to become engineers, but A wants to be an engineer, and B wants to be an engineer. They are different and cannot be put together. One of the invalid perceptions accepted by the majority is the perception of age as a success parameter. Sometimes we don't even personally accept it. It is just a social construct. It is like a long tradition passed down from generation to generation. Unfortunately, many never get to debunk this perception in their life. Success is a personal story and has nothing to do with your age. This has led many into depression and mental instability because they regarded themselves as a failure and wallowed in this thought. Success is peculiar to each person. That we are both women does not mean we should have achieved a feat at the same time. Or that we are both humans does not mean I have failed if I don't achieve something as early as you did. This is the way our minds have been conditioned, and it makes people make rash decisions, like a woman settling for an unhealthy relationship because she has to marry early.

First and foremost, you must be very confident in your forties. I mentioned earlier that it is the stage where there is a confidence boost. To further boost your mind, you must set your mind that your age does not determine your success. Your success is found in your life; how you are happy with the decisions you have made over your life. What is the essence of getting married to a person when you know you are not happy with it? To others, you have achieved something. You have succeeded in finding a party and taken away loneliness forever. But what it is to you is unhappiness, gloominess, and all sad feelings. The quality of your life should be the central focus at all ages, not what people consider as success.

When women talk and a conversation about age comes up, everyone wants to play a "guessing game." "How old do you think I am?" they asked. I thought it was immature to play that game. Knowing their age would not have changed a thing for me, other than maybe I would have a better idea of whether we could relate to each other. For example, I would have more things in common with someone closer to my age, as opposed to ten years younger. 20-year-olds, 30-year-olds, and 40-year-olds all grow up differently. They listen to different music, have different technology experiences, and have different priorities.

But maybe it is a generational thing. Older women, including my mother—though she has always been open about how old she is—have not had a problem with being asked their age. So, I find it strange that women my age and younger take offense when asked such a basic question. I wondered, "Are they afraid of being judged?" Then I realized that was it! It is a judgment issue. I do not see any reason that it is inappropriate to ask, "How old are you?" But maybe these women think that by knowing their age, the person asking would label them and lose interest in them.

Although it is my personal opinion that it is not inappropriate to ask about a person's age, I reckon with the fact that many people do not have that same opinion. It is okay to have a fear of being judged. From what I have been saying so far, this fear originates from the belief that at some ages, there are some achievements you must have had. It is as if it's a natural obligation for everyone to get some things done at a particular age. For instance, before 30, you are expected to have a degree. At 40, you should not be running all errands for yourself but should have the aid of your kids. These obligations are man-made. The natural order of life is that at all points in life, you should endeavor to be happy because things will try to get in the way. As we are saying, this perception of age and success is one of the hindrances to one's happiness. If you let it have its way, it will eat you down, and you will lose yourself to the fear of not meeting up.

This made me think even more about my fears and insecurities. I do not need a label! Why would anyone label me? I guess for the same reason, someone would judge me. I am not calling on you to hold the same opinion as me, but if, after reading this, you still feel it's inappropriate for someone to ask for your age, it's okay. What's not okay is if your feeling is premised on the fear that you might be judged. No, don't fear that. Be confident that you are living the life you want, the life you choose, and not the expectations people have of you. The reality is that people don't back up their expectations; they just expect. They do no more than expected, and it is not just you but every other person they know. Why concern yourself with someone who is not concerned about you but what they think you should be?

To what extent can we hide our age? If someone needs to know how old we are, they will find out. It is just a matter of time. The other day, a friend of mine told me a story about a wife who had lied to her husband about her age—she told him she was ten years younger than her actual age. If he had known the truth, would he not have married her? I mean, if I were a guy, I would be happy a woman looks so young at supposedly ten years older than I thought. I find it interesting that someone would go that far to disguise their age. Why are we so afraid of numbers? Again— people are labeling each other. People judge each other! So, in this couple's case, did the wife think her husband would be concerned that her ovaries were ten years older? I mean, he had already fallen for her looks. She has good genes. Would he think her ovaries were not up to par by being ten years older? Absurd. If a man cares that a woman is older, I call it simple immaturity!

The Beauty of a woman is not in a facial mode.
A woman's true beauty is in her soul. It is the caring that she gives and the passion that she shows.
The beauty of a woman grows with the passing years.[6]
—AUDREY HEPBURN

I have a few friends and acquaintances over 40 who have never been married and have no kids. A few are relaxed about it. The rest (the majority) are stressed out that they will never marry and think it is too late to have kids. Most have focused on getting their education and career and acquiring investments, but they have not yet found a better half. Now, they are scared

[6] Audrey Hepburn, www.quotefancy.com, Access date November 29, 2021, http://quotefancy.com/quote/3886/Audrey-Hepburn-The-beauty-of-a-woman-is-not-in-a-facial-mode-but-the-true-beauty-in-a.

they will be alone for the rest of their lives. They have done as they wish. What is important is why you do what you do. If you are doing it for societal acceptance or for the public to perceive you as successful, you will lack the confidence to defend your actions. But let's say you forgo marital life for a dream you have always had, and people judge you for your decision. You will not feel sad about their judgment. Instead, the joy and happiness you feel from doing what you want will fill in for you. Forty is not old. That's what people call it. Forty is a milestone where your life is a representation of your desires.

On the other hand, many successful people succeeded after turning 40. The list includes notable people such as Samuel Jackson, Martha Stewart, Ronald Reagan, Henry Ford, Abraham Lincoln, Reid Hoffman, Charles Darwin, Oprah Winfrey, and many more. If they had stopped believing at 40 that they could do what they did, the world would be different. But that success was just a timing thing. You cannot say that they did not try before. They just happened to make it after they turned 40. I do not think there was a preference to get married, start a family first, and then succeed. We cannot really know how exactly our life will plan out, but we should not be limited due to age.

Sure, maybe there are a few things you cannot do after 40, like be an astronaut or work for the CIA or the FBI, but almost everything else is possible in your 40s. Even if you dreamed of being a model, you still can. Maybe not Victoria's Secret model (they have an age limit there), but you can still be a model. You just have to prepare for your dream and act!

So, it is true. 40 is just a number. Chase your dreams. Do what you have always wanted to do! Create a bucket list and cross things off of it. Do it alone, or do it with your other half and your kids. Just do it! Do not care what others say. Do not even care when people ask you about your age… people will label and judge you, anyway. Do not stop living your best life because you are turning 40! And when they ask about your age, tell them you are fabulous at forty. First, they will wonder why it's fabulous – you have no obligation to explain why your life is fabulous -. It might even put them off their judgments against you. You must always remember that people's expectations of you at forty are just theirs. Live off your own expectations. That way, you might not find it inappropriate that someone is asking for your age. It will just be a normal inquiry. Age is just a number. Forty is not a limitation. Life begins at 40. Success is a combination of your work and time; each individual has time to succeed. Yours may be before 40 or after. But whatever it is, no one should let you feel you have failed at your age. Your success is the quality of your age. So, tell them you are 40 with grand confidence.

What can you take from this chapter?

The most important thing is how I feel, and not what my date of birth says. Do not lie about your age. Why? Because you would be lying to yourself first. Lying is not healthy. It will not get you anywhere. People will judge you no matter what you do. Other people's opinions do not matter. They are not living your life. You are living your life.

Journal Notes

_____

_____

_____

_____

_____

_____

_____

_____

_____

_____

_____

_____

_____

Ask yourself...

1. Do you feel old? Do you look old? Do you really feel your age?

    _____

    _____

    _____

    _____

    _____

    _____

2. Do you lie about your age? Why?

    _____

    _____

    _____

    _____

    _____

    _____

3. Do you care what others think about you? Why?

    _____

    _____

    _____

    _____

    _____

    _____

CHAPTER SIX

Acceptance

E ven in the oldest religion in the world, Hinduism, acceptance is a key to happiness. In psychological terms, acceptance is a person's assent to the reality of a situation, recognizing a process or condition (often a negative or uncomfortable situation) without attempting to change it or protest against it. There is a movement in psychology called "positive radical acceptance" that focuses on gratitude and resonating with positive things. Meaning you stop fighting reality when you stop responding with impulsive and destructive behaviors when things don't go your way. Basically, you stop reacting and do not allow that pain to become suffering. It works! Because of these techniques, people are improving their quality of life.[7]

---

[7] William Berry, "Acceptance: It isn't what you think," Last updated June 27, 2015,

Acceptance is undoubtedly a way to be happy. Although this I saw in a movie, there is so much sense in it. A dwarf was once asked why he did not seem to be worried and sad over the constant condemnations he received from people. He replied by saying that long before they started the condemnations, he had accepted himself for who he really was. He told himself what he was and what not, so when people started saying theirs, it did not matter because he had already accepted himself that way. Therein lies the simple explanation for acceptance.

You see, in life, when you deal with society generally, there has to be acceptance. An acceptance as to who you really are. That is why it is always advised that you conduct a self-discovery to know yourself for who you are and accept yourself before people try. As I said, there has to be acceptance in society. You either accept yourself or what others say. There's no third way about it and no standing on the fence.

A large number of people in society do not necessarily label you for ulterior motives or because of any bad intention; they are just constructed to say as they like. For instance, at 40, when people banter with you about not having a family of your own, it may not be because they want to hurt your feelings. Although some may do it for that reason, realistically, many don't do it for that reason. They have been influenced by the overriding traditions and thoughts that blur their logical

https://www.psychologytoday.com/us/blog/the-second-noble-truth/201506/acceptance-it-isnt-what-you-think.

reasoning. This can happen to anyone. All they know from living with their family and socializing with the community is that a woman should, at that age, have settled with a man and have children. I am bringing this to light to flaw the reasoning behind people's judgment towards other people.

Human judgments are so flawed because eight out of ten times, it is prompted by emotions and not logic. When they ask, "oh, you are forty and unmarried?" you feel bad about it without realizing their judgment was not reached on a logical appreciation of the circumstances surrounding your life but on the predominant belief which has clouded their reasoning. If there is something that has been in practice for ages and will still continue, it's that people will always have something to say about you. No matter what you do and how you do it, there will always be at least a judgment against it. Now, if there is something corresponding you must always have at heart is that you can never try to please everyone or get everyone on your side. There will always be at least one antagonist, also. Look at Jesus, though he is considered a great teacher and a good person, loved by many. In his own close circle, there was still someone who was against him. It is a natural order of life, and you must accept it! It's not that Judas Iscariot (the one against Jesus in his close circle) does not know about his wondrous nature. He was well aware of who Jesus was and even appreciated him. However, nature must take its course, and it took it through Judas. The events that occurred afterward revealed that Judas did not actually hate Jesus, but a feeling took over him, and he lost his reasoning.

That is just the situation. Nature takes its course through the people around you. You know life is like a series of tests. The moment you realize this, accept it and apply it to your life. Some things cannot just put you down. You must know and accept that people will look for things about your life to use against you, and you must be ready with the necessary knowledge. You must, firstly, find things about your life that you may grapple with when you get older. Accept what you are and will be, and find comfort and happiness in who you are.

For those of us turning 40, accepting that fact may be easier said than done. We should accept we will never be 25 ever again. If we try to do the things we did in our 20s, we fear being judged—and for a good reason. We live in a society in which people judge you no matter what you do. For example, if you have fun at 25, people say you are an irresponsible kid, too young, and dumb. If you are working at 25, you are too serious, and people say that if you keep at it for too long, it will be too late to live your life. If you are having fun at 45, people say you are irresponsible, not goal-oriented, and just want to party all your life. If you are not having enough fun at 45, they say you need to relax and enjoy life; otherwise, you may go crazy soon.

So, no matter what you do at whatever age, guess what? Society, friends, acquaintances, neighbors, mothers in your kids' school, whomever will judge you; it is just a nature of this world. You should accept that fact in all circumstances of your life and have fun, anyway! Unless they are paying your bills, why do you care what anyone else thinks? Do what you want. If you want to drive a convertible, wear trendy clothes, go Goth, or dye your hair five shades of purple, go for it. Do what makes you happy. Be who you are, accept who you are, and love who you are—inside and out. Live your life!

Understanding is the first step to acceptance,
and only with acceptance can there be recovery.[8]
—J. K. ROWLING

I know it sounds easy to say that you should accept the circumstances of your life and find happiness, but it is not as easy as it sounds. There will definitely be a war-like situation in your mind. That is because you will be in situations where you have to make a choice between what people say and what you think. It's the man-against-society war. It is not always easy. Although it is difficult, the important thing is that it is possible. It is possible to accept your decision instead of society.

---

[8] J. K. Rowling, www.goodreads.com, Access date December 5, 2021, http://www.goodreads.com/quotes/67454-understanding-is-the-first-step-to-acceptance-and-only-with.

Accept the fact that as you age, you change. Your body changes. Your look changes. I mean, come to think of it, it is bound to happen. No one can look young forever. So, you should learn to accept that. For a woman, this may be the hardest thing to accept. I mean, for one thing, our hair is not the same anymore. Every two months, we change our shampoo and conditioner, looking for something that works better for us. Our hormones trick us with ongoing minor changes. We gain weight faster; our metabolism is nowhere close to what it used to be. We try not to eat as much or only eat a little, and still, we gain weight. Our food intake changes. We find better foods and healthier ways to diet. But most of the time, we fail. It is only now that we realize we did not appreciate the way we looked in our 20s and 30s. We did not appreciate what we had … our beauty and youth. Instead, we looked around us, saw others we thought looked better, had more, or were more, and judged ourselves.

Now, in our 40s, we do the same—instead of appreciating how we look and accepting the fact we are aging, we find flaws. If you don't learn to accept yourself the way you are and appreciate yourself, you will end up having many regrets later. Ten years from now, we will look at a picture of ourselves from today and think, "Why didn't I love myself more? I was so much younger then. I looked great." So many women in their 60s look back at themselves 20 years ago and regret not loving themselves enough. We want to make sure we are not going to think the same when we are 60. That is what becomes of someone who doesn't learn to appreciate what they have at that moment. Then the saying that you don't know the value of something until you lose it becomes a practical reality of your life.

We need to learn to live life without or with little regrets. Yes, mistakes are bound to happen, but we can avoid repeating mistakes. If at the moment you cannot learn to appreciate how you are at 40, you will learn it later in your life, unfortunately, in a hard way. How do you go about this? Let's figure that out. One reason why you have a problem accepting yourself the way you are at 40 is that you are comparing yourself to another age. Comparison is not a bad thing. In fact, sometimes, it helps you bring out distinctive features in a thing or person that helps in making informed decisions. But when comparing, the subjects being compared should be proportionate to each other. In other words, what is being compared should be on the same level or have the same leverage.

A practical example is comparing the speed of an aircraft to a train. That is a very inappropriate comparison for many reasons. First of all, the components of an aircraft give it leverage that makes it the fastest mode of transportation. On the other hand, a train is not capable of that speed; its components are inadequate compared to the former. However, a more appropriate comparison will be between an airplane and a helicopter. These two mediums are proportionate to a very large extent. A comparison of both will not be regarded as absurd. The point I am bringing out is that it is absurd to compare your forties to your twenties because both ages are not the same. And as we have said earlier, as people age, so do changes occur in them. It is inappropriate for you to examine your life at 40 against your life at 20 or 30. There are different dispensations, and you must learn to accept that. We need to make better decisions right now and start loving ourselves right now. Accept the changes that will come with age and move forward. Take 40, accept the changes the way they come, and live them to the fullest. One sure thing is that you will never be forty again, just like you can never be twenty or thirty again. So why worry about the changes that occur? In fact, let me tell you a secret: you have so much worry about the changes occurring within you because of your countenance towards the changes. You must see them as something that will happen. And for the sake of your happiness, you must learn to accept them that way. If you see them as normal, they will just be normal to you when they occur. You will have no reason to worry about them.

One easy way to move forward and welcome the change (if you cannot do it alone) is to find someone who motivates you. Find a life coach, someone you look up to, someone positive who brings you joy and makes you smile every time you see or hear them. Suppose you are lucky enough to have them in your life, wonderful! Hold on tight! If not, that is where Facebook, Instagram, and the rest of social media come in.

So many people on social media are genuinely positive and happy and just want to pass this on to others. Look for them. Look for inspiration. We already spend so much time online. Why not find someone who will keep your spirits up? Do not look at the profiles, pages, and posts of twenty-year-olds and make yourself feel bad. If what they offer makes you feel insecure, do not follow them. But if someone motivates you, follow them. Get inspired. Let them show you what they can do for you. But do not compare yourself to anyone! Comparing is one of my biggest pet peeves. We compare ourselves and become unhappy. Why? Because we do not compare ourselves with someone who is the same age as us but looks older. We do not compare ourselves with someone who has less money than we do. We do not compare ourselves with someone less fortunate than us. We compare ourselves with someone younger-looking, richer, and more fortunate. This takes our happiness away. It causes us psychological pain. We focus on the wrong things!

We need to focus on the right things ... on the things we will look back on in ten years and realize: *we were all that and more*. We just did not appreciate ourselves enough. Why? Because we compare ourselves to others. A funny thing about comparison is that the someone else we are comparing ourselves to is comparing herself to someone else that is "better" than her (at least that is what she thinks) and that someone "better" is comparing herself to someone "even better." The comparisons go on and on. The list grows and grows! Do not include yourself in that list because it breeds unhappiness. Rather than compare, understand your age, accept the events that have occurred and will occur, and find happiness in your living. When we compare ourselves to others, we just want to be someone we are not and somewhere we are not. Why compare? We are all so different. We were all raised differently, and we all know and understand things differently. An alternative to comparing is to look up to someone who is doing something you want to do or someone you want to be like. If they can do it or be it—so can you! Let them uplift you and not make you feel bad.

How you decide to move forward in life is your choice. You have your ways, ideas, and opinions— all of them are stronger and more daring than when you were 25. You are more confident, mature, wiser, and loving than ever. Appreciate and praise yourself for the person you have become and continue improving daily.

For the longest time, I did not know that I did not love myself enough. I did not like how I dressed or that I had extra pounds I had to lose. Where was this coming from? I tried to lose weight. I tried to dress better. But all of that was just me not loving myself enough. If I had, I would have accepted who I was. Since I realized what was missing, a lot has changed. I recognized facts. I was not slender. Once I accepted that, I felt different about myself. I changed how I saw myself. "Even though I'm not skinny," I thought, "I should still love myself." I worked out. I committed to looking better and feeling better. That was my plan. I stuck with my plan. Now, everything around me has changed. I thought people cared about my weight, but they did not care about it. I was only trying to lose about thirty pounds, but every weight-loss journey is individual. It was hard—until I promised myself that I would love myself more no matter what outcome I got. When I made that promise, I knew I would not get results overnight, but I reminded myself daily that I needed to love myself. That worked for me. It made me realize what I have been missing and what I have been doing to myself. I was my biggest critic. I had to make sure I did not turn my self-criticism into self-deprecation. Sometimes we do it to be humorous, but more often, we are coming from a place of doubt and insecurity.

Regarding your life, no one can do anything better than you. If you must be happy, it is in your hands. If you must feel safe, it is in your hands, and so on. Even if other persons have influence as to decisions over your life, it is because you allowed it. At 40, you have not lost that will over your life to make yourself happy; it is still in your hands. Accept and stop comparing! Realistically, the comparison is a very unhealthy thing to do. You are just forty, just getting older, not getting worse in life. You need to assimilate thoughts that facilitate happiness in your life. Accept that at forty, you cannot live as a teenager or twenty or thirty. When you do that, it helps you shift concentration from the past and helps you live your forties to the best so that it will prevent you from having regrets in your later days.

What can you take from this chapter?

Accept changes as challenges. You can do it! Make yourself happy first. Then you can help and support others in finding their happiness. Appreciate yourself now, not in ten years. If you do not, you will regret it. Do not compare yourself to others. Have fun!

Journal Notes

_____

_____

_____

_____

_____

_____

_____

_____

_____

_____

_____

_____

_____

_____

Ask yourself...

1. Do you compare yourself to others? If yes, why?

   _____

   _____

   _____

   _____

   _____

   _____

2. Is there someone you look up to? Or, when you look up to someone, do you just feel bad about yourself?

   _____

   _____

   _____

   _____

   _____

3. If there is someone you look up to, do they do something you do not? Is it something you would like to do?

   _____

   _____

   _____

   _____

   _____

4. Do you get any inspirational ideas from the person(s) above? Is there something you can do that would inspire you?

_____

_____

_____

_____

_____

_____

_____

_____

_____

5. Is there anyone in your life who inspires or motivates you?

_____

_____

_____

_____

_____

_____

_____

_____

_____

CHAPTER SEVEN

Lies

I have always been proud of my age. I have never kept it a secret—if anyone asked me how old I was, I told them. But through the years, I have noticed that more women are secretive about how old they are. Why hide it? I have never understood it. The more I read about it, and the more women I speak to about it, the more I see why they do what they do.

Women lie about their age for many reasons, age discrimination being a major reason. When people find out a woman's age, their attitude toward that woman can change.[9] For example, age discrimination may prevent women from getting jobs, as companies hire younger women. Even though Employment Acts protect workers aged 40 and older from

---

[9] Precious Adesina, "Women Lying About Their Age Is Getting Old," Last updated December 3, 2018, http://www.refinery29.com/en-gb/why-women-lie-about-their-age.

discrimination in hiring, wages, and retention, women still feel discriminated against in hiring processes. That said, depending on the position you are applying for, some employers prefer experienced, responsible workers—because older workers do not have to be trained. They have gained many skills and solid experience and have achieved milestones. (So, there *are* some benefits to being older.)

Lying about age is not something that should be done because why hide it? But people have reasons. We already mentioned one, which is age discrimination. As a forty-year-old woman, you may still be attracted or get attracted to things that younger women dominate. That may prompt you to tell lies about your age. It is not unreasonable to tell such a lie, especially when you are not hurting someone in the process. It is not unreasonable to lie to someone that you are younger – people don't usually lie about being older - to get the person's attention or to get a privilege or a job. After all, we all have desires in this life, and this is what you want, but you lie to get it. But let us think about it, is lying worth it? Do you really have to lie to get what you want? The answers to these questions should help you determine if lying about your age is something you should do. I will give you two solid reasons why lying about your age is unnecessary.

First, lying is something almost everyone has done. To not say everyone entirely is an attempt to avoid a fallacy. However, the fact that it is a widely practiced act does not give encouragement to keep doing it. Even though everyone engages in it to an extent, it is not considered right. Lying, in its simple sense, is misrepresenting a state of fact. You say something is when it is not. Most of the time, people do it to avoid a consequence. Other times, people lie to get a benefit. Whatever the motive, when people lie, they do not present things the way they are.

There is always this thing people say that there is no greater sin; sin is a sin, and you would be punished for it. In the same vein, a lie is a lie. It is not a huge lie that makes someone a liar. In fact, there is nothing like a huge lie or a little lie. Once you misrepresent the state of matter, it is a lie. What I am trying to say is that although misrepresenting your age is just a little thing that hurts no one, it is still a lie. And that makes you a liar. I have mentioned earlier that everyone, at one point or the other, has told a lie about something. What do you expect the general attitude of people towards lying should be? Acceptance? Ignorance? You expect people not to judge people who lie because we all do it, right? Well, I'm going to burst your bubbles. That is not the people's reaction at all. People frown at lies as they frown upon other related acts. They see you as someone who is not honest and not brave enough to own up to things they are. You are viewed as a coward and an irresponsible person. Even though you have lied about one thing, they assume you cannot be honest with other things. Allow me to illustrate this short story I have witnessed. A little boy once joined a family. Things began to miss upon arrival of his presence. They suspected him, and he was caught red-handed. The boy was disciplined, and he promised never to do it again. Several weeks later, something went missing, and the only person that was suspected was the little boy. When asked, he denied even up till the point of crying. No one believed him. We know why: he has been caught stealing once and can only be the thief again. The little boy might not be the one who stole the last missing property, but he had a history of stealing, and people already see him in that light. If the little boy is not the person who took the property as he claimed, it will only take catching the real culprit before he can be relieved of all suspicions. Such, like others, is an unfair part of life. If you lie once, you are a liar for life in some people's eyes. When you are forty but tell people you are in your early thirties, and they figure that out later, they will cast doubts on almost everything you have ever presented to them. They will begin to ask whether you have been honest in anything, and you, on the other hand, will not feel too good because you only wanted to get a privilege. And now they are turning it on you because they think that you have lied about your age; hence, you could have lied about other things.

Think about it, is lying about your age worth these accusations that will follow? You are forty, and that's what you are. Instead of lying about it, embrace it and find the perfect spot for your age. The reason why you are most likely lying about your age is that you want to fit into a place, a thing, a group, or whatever it is. Now let's imagine you succeed in lying and fit in eventually. What happens when you are caught lying? There is always that possibility of being caught. You should always know that. You will never be trusted, but if you are ever trusted again, it will take a long time. You will lose the reputation or standing that you have gathered while you were there. And finally, you cannot fit it again because even you will not try again after being caught. What is now the essence of a building when it will all come down one day? If there is something salient you must know, lies do not sustain anything. Anything you build on lies will someday fall to the ground. When it falls, it will be like words spoken that cannot be returned to the mouth after coming out. Honesty is a solid foundation, while lying is the opposite.

A second reason why you should not lie about your age is that one lie leads to another. A lie does not end its race with just one lie; you have to keep it up. And you can only back up a lie with subsequent lies. Imagine a woman at forty who lies that she is thirty-three to join a women's club. They happily received her because they liked her, and she looks like she really maintains herself, seeing that she looks older than her age. They begin to interact, and as time goes on, she starts to make a contradiction due to her age. In order for her to retain her membership and to get them to still like her, she rebuffs it with another lie. Then maybe some other time, they find her age on her birth certificate in her documents, and she says again that it was a mistake. It doesn't end there; she keeps lying to cover up for her initial lie. Then probably someone who is very curious about these contradictions digs further without her knowledge and realizes that she lied about her age. Normally, her age does not disqualify her from being a member, but because she has lied several times to cover up for her age, they do not deem her worthy of the membership, and so she was removed. The moral is that whatever you build on lying will tremble to the ground. It may hold for a while but not forever. And when you lie once, there is an almost irresistible urge to keep lying about that same thing. You may have decided that it is only your age you want to lie about, but because of that one lie, you will have to lie about other things just so they can correspond and cast doubts off people's minds. The circle goes on like that until it eventually ends, and not in your favor.

Women who lie about their age—in job interviews, for example—are not underachievers. They are simply scared of discrimination. But remember, employers will find out how old you are; you do not want to start a new job with a lie! You just have to believe that the right position will arise and that the right employer will hire you.

*

So, knowing all this may cause issues at some points, why do women still lie about their age? As noted earlier, we consider it impolite to ask a woman how old she is. But as I said, why should we feel ashamed of our age? Are we afraid of being judged or being compared to others? Are we concerned other women look better than we do or that their genes are better than ours? Some things we can control, some we cannot—it is all thanks to natural selection. On a proper evaluation of things, the consequences of lying weigh heavier than what you benefit. So, we must accept what we are and roll with it. That said, there are many things you can change about yourself nowadays, from wearing contact lenses to changing your hair color and from exercising to dressing a certain way to hide your flaws or show your perfections. But we need to work with it, not against it. We need to put time and effort into ourselves!

Why is age such a taboo? I have heard stories about men who have broken off their engagements when they find out that the woman they planned to marry is older than them. Wow. Does that mean he did not love her to begin with? But why lie to your betrothed about your age in the first place? If you do, it means you start your married life based on a lie—not a clever idea. Hey, I would break up with that lying woman, too! But what is a single older woman to do? Just lie for the rest of her life?

There are a lot of people out there who lie about their age and I think it does us all a disservice. It cannot all be over when you hit 30. That would be rubbish.[10]

—SOPHIA ELLIS BEXTOR

Why can't society appreciate women more, despite their age? Because our parents bring us up to judge people instead of accepting people for who they are. It starts there. Realists point out that if you want to live in this world, you must accept the facts. Idealists state you can change the world if you take the right action. We cannot change the fact that we are turning 40! We need to change our expectations, accept the facts, and make our life plans based on that. No matter how you try to hide it, nothing will change how old you are. Nothing! We can get on with our lives as soon as we make peace with that.

Being older is not bad! Being older means you are more experienced and wiser. You should be proud of that. Older women can tell who is fake and who is real; who is lying and honest; who is compassionate, and who is full of themselves. We gain that magical knowledge through our own experiences and the experiences of people in our life. Life does not end at thirty or twenty. There is also life to live at forty, fifty, and even sixty. There is life to live at every point in time. You may not see that because your eyes are fixed solely on the past. Look at your environment and your life. There are perfect things to do at forty. You don't have to lie to take yourself back. It will not account well because it will come bouncing on you as a heavy rock. But all you can do is accept that you have lived those ages

---

[10] Sophie Ellis-Bextor, www.brainyquotes.com, Access date December 10, 2021, https://www.brainyquote.com/quotes/sophie_ellisbextor_428884.

in the past and prepare to live for the now. When you get your mind fixed on that, you will figure out the amazing things you can do at your age that you never imagined. The point is, there is really no need to lie. You are forty, and lying does not take that from you. Whatever happiness you derive from the lie will be short-lived because it just can't last long.

Your self-acceptance and self-love come first in life. Most of us do not realize that we do not accept ourselves—meaning we do not love ourselves enough. Self-love and self-acceptance give us assurance and confidence. Accepting the fact that you are turning 40 is the first step. The second step is letting everyone else in your life accept that fact, too. If they have an issue with it, they are not meant to be in your life. Remember—no one else's opinion matters.

What can you take from this chapter?

Be proud of your age. Love your age. It is evidence of your experience and your expertise. Love yourself. Practice self-love. There are many ways to get there. Research and find a way that works for you.

Journal Notes

Ask yourself...

1. Are you proud of yourself and who you are?

    _____

    _____

    _____

    _____

    _____

    _____

2. Do you remind yourself how wonderful you are each day?

    _____

    _____

    _____

    _____

    _____

3. Do you lie about your age? Why?

    _____

    _____

    _____

    _____

    _____

    _____

CHAPTER EIGHT

What to Expect

Getting older is something that cannot be avoided. That's why in some ways, you should expect it and prepare for its coming. Why do we notice we are turning a certain age? The most common reason people bring themselves to the consciousness that they are getting older is the changes in physical appearance. We look at ourselves and exclaim, "Oh, I am getting older!" then we begin to think of the other changes that have been happening within us. When I turned 35, I saw wrinkles on my face. My metabolism slowed down. I got tired faster. I could not party late anymore—in fact, I dreaded any outing past 8:00 p.m. I chose movie nights in my pajamas over late-night parties. I could not function the next day if I did not sleep at least six hours at night. If people had the choice, they would choose to be young forever because these changes are not always favorable.

So many changes take place as we age. Sometimes we do not even know what to pay attention to at first. Brain fog. Random facial hair growth. Gray hair. Hair loss. Hot flashes that can last a decade! Vision loss and blurry vision. Dizziness. Urinary dysfunction. Water retention and bloating. Heart palpitations. Dry skin. Acne. Sleep disruption and disturbances. Night sweats. Menstrual changes. Anxiety. Short-term memory loss, difficulty concentrating, and fuzzy thinking. Difficulty multitasking. Fatigue. Mood swings. Anger. A sense of urgency … all these are symptoms of reaching the dreaded 40! If you are experiencing these changes, you are not alone. I never thought about even five of these issues five years ago—now, about one-third are on my everyday list. One of my biggest things has been headaches. They come and go, last for days, do not return for two weeks, and then return again. Holy smokes.

And that is not all—there are many more signs of aging, among them entering perimenopause, which begins several years before menopause. This is the time your body makes a natural transition to menopause, marking the end of your reproductive years. And that is important. There are more to the changes you will experience physically, mentally, and even spiritually. More changes to your environment, mindset, and family. We cannot reverse time, that's one thing for sure, and you cannot stop time. Time must keep moving, and you must age older. These changes are bound to happen to every woman as they age. You may not experience all, and even this list is not exclusive. Therefore, you must create an expectancy in your mind. You must always have it in mind that this time is bound to come and own up to the circumstances. It is inevitable. The only way out is to embrace it and live the best way for your life.

One of the biggest concerns about aging I hear from other women is about kids. We all think we will not have any more kids after 40. It is true that after 40, your egg quality and quantity goes down.[11] It does not actually mean you cannot have kids after 40 or at 40. Although the chances are very low because, as mentioned earlier, your egg quality has reduced, conceiving is still possible. If you are planning to have a child after 40, remember that your energy levels for childcare will not be the same as if you have children in your mid-20s or even your 30s. These days, many women have kids in their late 30s and early 40s.[12] The technology is so advanced now that you can even still have children at fifty. Many busy professional women freeze their eggs and use surrogate mothers. If you expect to do that, do it early. That way, your eggs will not go to waste, and you can donate them or discard them if you change your mind. It is all up to you. Remember, you alone are in charge of your body and your life! You just have to decide if

---

[11] acog.org, https://www.acog.org/womens-health/faqs/having-a-baby-after-age-35-how-aging-affects-fertility-and-pregnancy#.

[12] Gretchen Livingston, "They're waiting longer, but U.S. Women today more likely to have children than a decade ago," www.pewresearh.org, Last updated January 18, 2018, https://www.pewresearch.org/social-trends/2018/01/18/theyre-waiting-longer-but-u-s-women-today-more-likely-to-have-children-than-a-decade-ago/.

you care about what people will say (and you should not care). This is your life. You decide what you want your future to be and what changes you will make along the way. People will talk either way, so why base your decisions and plan your life on what others think? Just do what makes you happy.

There is so much emphasis on doing what makes you happy at this stage because that should be your central focus. You have probably lived your earlier years trying to make things work for yourself physically, emotionally, mentally, and spiritually; almost everyone did that. You should have these expectations. Really, you must expect that changes will occur. These changes will want to fall you into a crisis, but you must balance your life and prioritize that which will benefit your life. Do you know why we should expect these changes that occur from the forties? Having an expectation reduces the burden you feel regarding those changes. Let me explain further.

Regarding disappointment, advisably you should not expect too much from people. For instance, don't expect your friend to always be there for you at every moment. Or don't expect that a close friend of yours can ever betray you. Normally, you should expect these things; your very close friend should not betray you. Also, your friend, who is more than an acquaintance, should be there for you when you need them, although not every moment. However, the realities of this world reveal that no one - whether your family or a friend or best friend - is above making mistakes or disappointing another. That is why they advise that you should not expect so much from them so that when it happens – if it does happen – you will not feel as much hurt as you would have felt if you had expected them not to do what they did. Let's say your birthday is approaching. You have a best friend you have known for seven months, and you expect her to buy you a gift for your birthday. Your birthday came, and she didn't give you anything asides from her full presence for the whole day at your house. This made you feel so disappointed because you had thought that at least if you were to get a gift for your birthday, it would come from your best friend. This led to you doubting if your best friend sees you the way you see her or if she values your relationship as you value it. Now, let's consider the other side. Imagine if you were so full of cheer the weeks preceding your birthday that you did not even consider getting a gift from your best friend. First, if she gives you a gift, eventually, you will be delighted that she thought of gifting you something. Second, if she does not give you a gift, you may just wonder why. But it will not hurt you as much as it did in the first instance because you were not expecting her to give you anything here. You were busily preoccupying your mind with your life and how your birthday would be. That is the thing with expectations; they either reduce or increase disappointment. That is simply why you should expect that your life will not be the same as when you were a teenager, in your twenties, or even in your thirties. When you have these expectations, it prepares your mind against what you are yet to face. And you know what happens to someone who faces a challenge prepare? (The person has a high chance of scaling through.)

"

Studies show that women 40 and older tend to be more confident and know what they like and need than in their earlier years. There is a decrease in dependence and self-criticism and an increase in self-confidence and decisiveness.[13]
—**GOOGLE SEARCH: "What to expect when you turn 40."**

The reason why it's like that is that you know what you want and no longer have to depend on people anymore because, over the year, your experiences have been building you. You have learned to attach; you just cannot be attached as you used to be. Usually, as people grow older, their dependency rate reduces because they are becoming sufficient to an extent in the areas where they depend on people. This does not exclude women. At forty, you would have been engaged in a job or trade that is taking care of your bills, thereby making you independent of your parent's finances, and so on. Your confidence boosts because there is certainty. You have heard

---

[13] Deb Schilling, "You're Turning 40-Embracing Both Physical and Emotional Changes at this Milestone Birthday," www.mankatoclinic.com, Last updated February 9, 2015, http://www.mankatoclinic.com/youre-turning-40.

that a fool at forty is a fool forever, right? It is because that age is the generally recognized landmark for maturity. At this age, you must have had experiences and garnered knowledge that prevents you from making your past and improving your life, therefore, causing developments.

One of the best things I experienced when I turned 39 was realizing I was happier than ever before with who I am. I am more confident and less stressed than I was even three years ago. One thing is for sure: we are not only getting older but also getting wiser. Have you noticed that older people are sought for advice? And I'm sure you know the reason why. Wisdom is something of knowledge and its application. Being wise just does not involve having accurate knowledge about something. It also knows how to apply that knowledge. The reason why older people are regarded as wiser is that the longer they have spent in the world, the more they have gathered knowledge, and from their experiences, they know how best to apply the knowledge. For instance, an older teenager who has started her period will know how to instruct a younger teenager who has just started her period. She will have accurate information on how to calculate periods, wash up during periods, eat, or exercise to do during periods. And that is just simply because she is older, and that status accounts for more experience and knowledge. Being forty is not the oldest, but it is surely older than twenty or thirty. As a forty woman, you have the pride of being wiser. You know more than the younger folks to a large extent, which gives you a medium of an adviser or someone that can be looked up to for support. We discussed the changes that will occur when you get older, and you should expect them. They mostly consist of unfavorable changes, but here lies a delightful one. You should expect that people will look up to you. They will want to learn from you how you managed your life, family, friends, work, etc. they perceive you – as they perceive other older people – to be more knowledgeable, and they will also like to see from your perspectives.

Sure, the symptoms of aging are sometimes hard to manage, and everyone is different. I have some symptoms. You have other symptoms, and someone else has others. Some have more symptoms. Some have fewer.

If your symptoms are many or unmanageable, or you have health concerns, see your doctor. Do not wait. There is a reason for health insurance, so use it. Even if you worry about something, it is better to be safe than sorry, right? Even if there is something worrisome, you are better off catching it early. Talk to your doctor about what you should and should not do, on a medical level, to ease the discomfort of aging. If you want to read up on what to expect regarding physical changes, there are many books on the changes a woman goes through after 40. (I list some in the Reading List at the end of the book.) Ask your doctor which ones are right for you. Self-care should be your priority.

Getting committed to streamlining my self-care was key for me. For example, after having two kids and multiple epidurals, my back was bothering me a lot. I had headaches daily. I did not know if these were all signs of getting older or if something else was up. I went for chiro, Physical Therapy, acupuncture, X-rays, and MRIs ... I tried it all. My shoulder was bothering me from carrying my heavy babies. I got my shoulder and back stronger, and that made me feel better. I reduced my coffee and tea intake, which helped me manage my headaches. My doctor ran blood tests to ensure my hormone levels were normal, and some of my vitamin levels were not up to par. My Vitamin D was low, so I took Vitamin D and other supplements. My hair was not growing as fast after I had my second daughter as it did after my first daughter. So, as I mentioned earlier, I took collagen and Hairtamins, and those helped a lot. These are just a few of the things I have experienced in the past few years that made me realize I am not 25 anymore! And that is okay. As I said, aging means becoming not only older but wiser.

We are all smart enough now to accept the negatives and focus on the positives and all the good things that come with turning 40. We can look at the exciting things in life and enjoy every moment we have with those who matter. We have gotten this far in learning who we are and what we are worth, and what those people we choose to keep around us are worth to us, too. The bad things are no longer a focus. We have learned to love ourselves.

What can you take from this chapter?

We all will feel "our age" eventually. Do your routine physicals every year. You have nothing to lose, and you may prevent something that can be bigger than you want. Accept changes and adapt to them. Be happy. Be grateful. Experiment, find your way to accept the changes, and work with them..

Journal Notes

Ask yourself...

1. Are you content as an individual? Physically and emotionally? (If you are not, what can you do to improve your health? Write bullet points on what you can do to improve the level of comfort and ease in your life.)

   _____

   _____

   _____

2. Did you accept the fact that you and everyone around you will age? (There is nothing we can do to change that!)

   _____

   _____

   _____

   _____

3. Are you grateful for who you are and what you have done so far to be who you are in your own body? Do you take care of yourself (eat well, exercise, drink water, etc.)?

   _____

   _____

   _____

CHAPTER NINE

Fear

Fear is a very common social term because we all fear something. We hear about midlife crises, but no one talks about their midlife fears. But the 40 mark seems to separate us from "carefree" thinking to "worrying about it all" thinking. Our anxieties lead to social and personal life disturbances because, currently, in our lives, we focus on our fears. For me, my fear of aging was not like a fear of spiders, snakes, or grasshoppers. It was deeper than that. I did not want to discuss certain things; I did not want to read up on those things. I tried to avoid these thoughts as they came into my head, brushing them off, trying to think of something else....

But once I faced facts, I realized I feared death and getting old. The more women I talked to around my age, the more I realized (once again) that I was not alone. As I said earlier, I wrote this book because I felt lonely in my fears. I searched and searched for answers, but no book gave me simple "You are not alone" or "You are not going crazy" reassurance. I could not connect to anything "out there." But here is the good news—we are not alone in going through this 40-craziness. It is just that no one talks about it. The fear of dying is not only associated with women entering their forties; people generally begin to have this fear when they get older. Not everyone feels this fear, though. Some people live the whole of their life without worrying about or fearing death. Somewhere in this book, I mentioned something crucial about getting older. I said that the older you get, there are two sides to it: the positive and the negative. The positive is that you are celebrating another year of being a champion – this life is a whole battle itself, and people who are able to pull through each year are champions. The negative aspect of it is that you are closer to death; you are closer to leaving the world. As your age increases, your time on earth decreases. If there is one inevitable thing, which everyone knows it is, it's that death will happen to all. The rich, the poor, the middle class, the white, the black, men, women, and the entire earth will be a victim of death one day. Children do not die as often as adults do. Older people are the ones that are more prone to death. Children who die probably die as a result of one ailment or accident. But it is generally known that adults are more likely to die. The older you get, the most likely you are to die. That is why the fear of death exists largely only amongst older people. It is very rare to find a teenager or a person in her twenties worrying about death or having fears originating from death. However, on the other hand, adults from age forty and above have this fear and worry the most because their chances are higher.

I would have said fear is an integral part of life, but it is not in a positive way. Also, I would have said death is an integral part of life, again, not in a positive way. Because fear is something that comes in people based on their perception of things, fear is not an invalid feeling. Fear is very normal. At one point in life, we have one fear or the other. Sometimes, fears motivate our actions. Fear pushes us to do some things we might not have done. Fear has led many to do positive and negative things, beneficial and detrimental, and so on. After a long time of ignoring my thoughts, I realized, "I have to address this." The more I tried to avoid my thoughts, the more they came into my head. For me, getting older triggered life's biggest questions. Being afraid can put one in a position where everything overwhelms you. It all boiled down to me being afraid of losing something or someone. But I feared losing my family members—*What would happen to them?* I was scared something might happen to me—*What if I die tomorrow? What will happen to my daughters?* Then there was the fear of not seeing someone again. *What if something happened to them?* Yes, I understand that when people die, their loved ones manage and move on with their lives. But it made me realize that when we say goodbye to someone, we should not just say "Goodbye." We need to mean it … what if it is your last time seeing that person?" Just yesterday, someone forwarded a video to me made by Will Smith about that topic. It made me think about the many things we take for granted in our lives—getting older is just one of them.

The fears that are associated with getting older, if not put in check, can make someone live an almost miserable life. That is because this fear causes you to do deep thinking as you have never done before and causes you to critically evaluate your life, which may almost lead to depression. Aside from the fear of death, some other fears include the fear of underachievement. We have talked about this extensively in a previous chapter. Women compare their lives with other lives at this age and conclude that they have not achieved much like their peers of the same age; hence they are underachievers. They may not necessarily call themselves that, but it is how they feel. They live in fear that they have been wasting their days because they have not done as much as others. For emphasis' sake, I will recap.

This fear of not doing well enough at your age or not achieving as much as others have achieved is not an invalid one. As I said, society has constructed our minds to make us believe that a success story applies generally. Thus, what a woman has achieved is expected of another woman. But I must reiterate success is individualistic in nature. You may be of the same gender and age it does not mean that you must achieve the same things. At this age, women are preoccupied with what they see other women achieving at their age that they haven't. It is wrong to do that. You may feel this way and have this fear clouding your emotions and reasoning, but you should debunk it. Live your life the way that seems best. Achieve what you want and not what you see other women achieving. Women should deal with this fear of achievement because it should not have a place. At every point in life, the quality of your life is always paramount. Would you rather spend your forties worrying about the things you see other women achieving and you haven't achieved? Or would you spend it on developing yourself and doing the things that help you grow and be happy? After all, death may come anytime soon, and it would not matter how many things you achieved; you will die anyways. (sorry this is coming as raw as it sounds, but it is the truth and not meant to frighten you) It means you have to choose how to live the rest of your life, worrying in fear or being happy.

As for fear of death, some fear for themselves and also fear for their loved ones, like me. It is not easy to think of losing someone because you will always have memories of things you intend to do with them. The fear of death can make you lose yourself if you do not control it. Death itself is a sad and painful event. I am sure if people had the choice, they would choose never to die. The sad reality is that when someone dies, they no longer have a chance in life. The only thing you have of them are memories you shared while they were alive. Someone once said the most painful thing about missing a dead person is not that you miss the things you did together but that you miss the things you would have done together if they were alive. As you get older, this fear of leaving the world and losing someone grapples you. It is normal for that to happen. But you really cannot live the rest of your life that way. In one of the early previous chapters, we talked about expectations. The fact that we know that death is inevitable, for me, is a strong reason to expect death. I should differentiate that to expect death is different from fearing death. When you expect death, it means you have your mind prepared for the event, and you most likely do not care when it takes its toll on you. However, when you fear death, you are scared of death happening. It means you are not prepared to have something like that happen to you.

There is something fear does. Fear holds people in subjection. When you are held by the fear of losing your life or your loved one as you get older, you will fail to realize the simplicity of the matter. The truth is your days are getting shortened, and death must happen. So instead of being subjected to the torture of the thoughts of death, accept the reality and live the rest of your life happily. If you fail to control the fear, it will control you and hinder you from seeing what you should have done. The reality is that death must happen, so why bother about it? Why worry over something you cannot control? You have a life that you can absolutely control. Take charge of that and worry no more about losing to death. Let me borrow the words of the Bible, "how many of you can add to your days by worrying?" That is it; worrying simply takes your time, peace, and happiness. Get off the worry and overcome the fear!

One of the greatest discoveries a man makes, one of his great surprises, is to find he can do what he was afraid he could not do. [14]
—HENRY FORD

Why is it scary to get old? Because we hear sad stories, we do not plan for old age (but we do plan for parties), and we do not want to die alone. We do not expect old age to come around so fast; we think we have a long way to go. But when 40 hits, it hits hard. None of my family ever spoke to me about their fear of getting old and all that comes with it. So, why have I thought about it so much? Why am I so different? They are not scared. Why am I? What did I do that they did not? Did they age better than me? Why are they not afraid of death?

---

[14] Henry Ford, www.brainyquote.com, Access date November 29, 2021, http://www.brainyquote.com/quotes/henry_ford_133753.

Death is inevitable. We all know that. There is nothing we can do to stay on this earth forever. No one knows how long we have to live, so the best way to live is to enjoy each day to the max. So, having thought about that for a while, I realized, "Well, I can fear death and getting old, or I can make the best out of the time I have." It was a simple decision. But creating a plan to get to my goal of making the best of the time I have was tough. Trust me, I had days when I forgot to think that way, but I have learned to reroute my train of thought. Now, I live every moment and make the most out of every day in any way possible. That does not mean every day is perfect. But I have learned to be grateful for each day. I find at least one thing to be grateful for and call it a good day. Trust me, when you do this, you wake up the next day with a smile on your face, and you choose to think happy thoughts. You are grateful you woke up and grateful your day is going to unfold before you. (Later in the book, I describe my way to daily happiness and how I enjoy every day as it comes.)

It is crazy how some things we hear daily do not get to us until bang—it hits you. For example, how often have you heard people say, "Live each day like it's your last day?" I never gave that adage much thought until I realized the things changing in my life. I am not worried about impressing people anymore. I am more concerned about having a wonderful day and practicing gratitude. I am not worried about which party to go to anymore. I am concerned about the quality of life my family and I have. Taking care of my family and being happy and grateful have become the most important things in my life. Like I said earlier, dying means no more chances. That means each day you wake up alive is a chance to do what you did not do the previous day, to put yourself first again, and to make yourself happy again. You should not fear the things that are not within your power when there is the option of overlooking the fear and living your life. It may be good sometimes to think about death. I mean thinking about the end of your life of losing someone dear to you. This may open you to things you want to do before death. For instance, when you begin to fear death, it may make you realize the many things you want to do about life that you have not done. In that manner, thinking about death is positive because it opens you up to things you can do to improve your numbered days on earth.

The most important thing is that you are happy as you get older because whether you think of death or not, it will happen. Instead, preoccupy your mind and your life with thoughts that will improve the quality of your life. This is what we all should do, and not worry about sad things and people in our life. Live your life to the fullest!

What can you take from this chapter?

You are not alone; You are not going crazy. Enjoy every moment of your life; live each day. Do not let fear control you or your life. Appreciate those who matter in your life.

Journal Notes

Ask yourself...

1. Do you accept your fears? If not, why not? What can you do to accept them and live peacefully?

_____

_____

_____

_____

_____

2. Do you have a plan for all your worries and fears? If you do not, create a plan today!

_____

_____

_____

_____

_____

3. Remind yourself to live each day. Do not wait for tomorrow.

_____

_____

_____

_____

_____

CHAPTER TEN

Millennials' Problems

While searching for answers about aging and turning 40, I read an article about the problems we Millennials face today.[15] Student debt is one of the biggest problems in this country. Since most jobs require a Bachelor's degree, Millennials have no choice but to get the degree. Still, having a Bachelor's degree does not guarantee a job, as most hirers want applicants to have experience. Hence, unemployment is the second big problem for Millennials. Unemployment is always frustrating, but in the past three years, the pandemic has increased unemployment rates across all generations. Lower wages and a less-than-desirable job environment go hand in hand, as Millennials are particular about what they earn and

---

[15] Ketura Bursten, "7 Serious problems Millennials face today," www.therapyinbeverlyhills.com (blog), Access date December 10, 2021, https://www.therapyinbeverlyhills.com/7-serious-problems-millennials-face-today/.

with whom they work. We change our jobs yearly (or every few years) to advance our careers. And with a low income and an unstable career, it is difficult to keep up with rising costs of living—including costs for housing and medical care.

These problems of student debts and unemployment are not only peculiar to the millennials. The generation before and after also face the same problems. Taking a student loan is justifiable in light of the expected benefit. It is hoped that by the time you finish your education and get a job, you will be able to pay the debt from the salary. Then it leads to the second problem; there is no job. You are now left with a debt to be paid and other responsibilities to shoulder. Due to the high unemployment rate, sometimes, this debt lingers until you are forty or more.

Dealing with debts is not as easy as it sounds. That is because debts are not the only thing you have to finance. Other areas of your life need financing as well. It is often difficult to carry debts and other bills that must be settled. For instance, even as a young adult, you are independent to an extent. That means you may already have your apartment, which means rent bills. In the apartment, there are other bills to take care of, which include all utility bills. Personally, you need groceries. You need clothes, and so on. Then there will be debt on its own, which you must take care of compulsorily. These bills all sum up to frustrating people. It is very common among millennials. This situation worsens when you don't have a job that pays off. The struggle hits so hard that it sometimes gets to people mentally.

This means that, more than ever, you need to be financially stable. Responsibilities increase as people get older. The major reason why is that older people no longer depend on their parents or family for financial support. In fact, it is now you who would be relied on for support. Your responsibilities will not care whether you have an adequate job or a job at all. It stays and even increases sometimes. The only way out is to find a way out of a financial crisis. You need to pay debts and take care of yourself and your family, if possible.

The COVID-19 pandemic came as a disaster to people. It wrecked many people primarily because some business operations had to be halted. Some businesses did not recover from the pandemic. Many workers were laid off from their workplaces. People struggled because of the negative impacts of the pandemic. However, there is a positive perspective of the pandemic that affects finances. If there is one thing that the pandemic did apart from its other negative impacts, it is that the pandemic exposed the inefficiency of many businesses. The pandemic caused an economic crisis, but not everyone was affected. There are some sets of persons that, even during the pandemic, were making money. The inefficiency exposed by the pandemic is that some businesses cannot survive physical lockdowns. Due to the directives by State governments to curtail the spread of the virus, many, I mean a lot of businesses had to stop operating till the directive was lifted. It meant that the business could only survive in a physical environment.

Meanwhile, we are in a dispensation where almost everything is now digital. After the lockdown, many businesses adapted to the exposition. They looked for ways to ensure their business could thrive without physical operation. Others did not need to return to their job because, during the pandemic, they figured out how you can make money without going to a job.

It is no new knowledge that we live in a digital age. Almost every activity is conducted through digital means. People now sell digitally, people now school digitally, and people do almost everything now digitally. Money is now made digitally as well. It is a sure way to escape unemployment and get enough finances to cater to your responsibilities, debts included. Most of these jobs are done from home. So, in the comfort of your home, you can make enough to care for your needs.

The most common of these jobs is affiliate marketing. It involves you selling on behalf of others. You do not need to have a product to sell. You are just a middleman. Another is blogging/vlogging. People now sit in the comfort of their homes writing about their experiences or on a particular subject where they are knowledgeable. Others include using one skill or the other to make money. Some of these skills include video creation/editing, graphics designing, copywriting, and so on. These skills have been remarked to be utilized by people to make a lot of money. The interesting thing about these jobs, apart from those requiring a skill like graphics design, is that they have no experience requirement and no age limitation. Businesses are conducted digitally, so it is unimportant if you can walk efficiently to your workplace. These jobs have replaced the order of office work such that it is almost people who have a passion for office jobs are still at it. The digital world has been embraced for financial purposes, and it is good news for you as well because you can embrace it as well. You just find the area where you think you will function very effectively and invest in it. Then you get your millennial problems of debts and unemployment solved.

There is one important thing I should let you know. Having a job does not mean you will be able to pay up all your debts. It will take you disciplining yourself before you can do that. You can, for instance, challenge yourself to get only the things you need until your debts are paid off. If you do not discipline yourself enough, you will find that despite working, you still have debts piled up. That is because people sometimes don't restrict their buying to things they need but also go as far as getting things they want when there are other pressing needs.

Caring for aging parents is another challenge and responsibility many of us were not ready for—many Millennials take care of their parents, and some have even moved back to their parent's house to take care of them.

Parental care is one responsibility that children cannot turn a blind eye to. When you are forty, either of your parents will be at least around sixty years and above. They are getting to the point where they need to be dependent. The circle that existed when you were younger will now be repeated, only that the roles are now being switched. While you were younger, you depended on your parents for food, shelter, clothes, education, and so on. Now, they are older and probably incapable of being active as they were, and also health issues kick in. Then they will now depend on you, and as a responsible child, you must take up that responsibility. Depending on the circumstances of the case, the responsibility may not be heavy, but whatever it is, you must balance all your responsibilities in a way that none is suffering from a lack of attention. If it gets overwhelming for you, get assistance. In the event that you are not the only one who is to shoulder the responsibility, don't overact by taking it all up. Get all the needs you need so that you don't abandon your personal responsibilities in the process of taking care of your parents.

But of all the concerns Millennials deal with, mental health is the toughest.[16] With all that is happening around us and around turning 40, we have to make sure we stay sane and figure out how to manage our stress.

---

[16] Gretchen Frazee, "Millennials report more stress than older Americans during Pandemic." www.pbs.org, Last modified August 8, 2020, https://www.pbs.org/newshour/health/millennials-report-more-stress-than-older-americans-during-pandemic.

*

Why are we so different from Generation X-ers, the generation before us? Statistics show that three out of ten Gen X-ers have Bachelor's degrees, whereas four out of ten Millennials have a Bachelor's degree. So, education-wise, both generations are similar. But statistics also show that where Generation X-ers are adaptable, Millennials are sometimes thought to be lazier and less interested in keeping their jobs.[17] But fifty-one percent of Millennials own (or intend to own) a business—so we Millennials are not lazy, we just want to make our own rules.[18]

Millennials, and the generations to follow, are shaping technology. This generation has grown up with computing in the palm of their hands. They are more socially and globally connected through mobile Internet devices than any prior generation. And they do not question; they just learn.[19]
—BRAD D. SMITH

---

[17] The Council of Economic Advisers, "15 Economic Facts About Millennials," White House, Last updated October 2014,
https://obamawhitehouse.archives.gov/sites/default/files/docs/millennials_report.pdf.
[18] Melanie Hanson, "College Graduation Statistics," Last modified August 9, 2021,
https://educationdata.org/number-of-college-graduates.
[19] Brad Smith, www.picturequotes.com, Access date November 29, 2021,
http://www.picturequotes.com/millennials-and-the-generations-that-follow-are-shaping-technology-this-generation-has-grown-up-quote-1008269.

Given all the obstacles we Millennials face, our only way to get ahead is to debt-finance our lives—which means getting deep into credit card debt. Credit card debt can be our best and our worst friend. Almost everyone in the USA is in debt. First, we get into debt to get an education that takes at least six years, and then we spend another six years getting out of debt, sometimes longer. Credit card companies make it "convenient" to get into their little debt game. And we do not mind playing the game at all—until we max those credit cards out and have a tough time paying them off. I have always wished that universities and colleges would provide credit card education at the same time they accept tuition fee payments. That should be a college requirement, like a health class in high school. Students would be so much more informed about how to manage the everyday stresses of finances, and by the time they are out of college, they will know what to expect and be prepared to manage their money. As Nelson Mandela once said, "Education is the most powerful weapon we can use to change the world."[20]

Get out of debt a.s.a.p.—it is a trap. There are a lot of debt consolidation companies out there that will combine your debt so you have one payment. I got into that credit card game, and it was hard to get out. I just wish I had known how the system worked. I would never have gotten myself into it. Education is the key! There are so many books, so much material, and so

---

[20] Nelson Mandela, https://www.pinterest.com/pin/543668986245093192/.

much guidance from people who went through the same thing and who will tell you how to manage your finances. Just keep reading and learning. If you have a credit card, pay it off each month. If you cannot pay your credit card off at the end of the month, you cannot afford what you are buying and should not be buying it. When it comes to finances, financial education is very important. There is a secret I figured out when I was reading a blog post. Making a lot of money does not equate to having a lot of money. You will think that ought to be the case, right? Like, if someone makes a lot of money monthly, that person should definitely have a lot of money. Well, that is not the case. Proper money management is what makes people have money. That is why a person who earns less can have more than someone who earns higher. I was talking with someone one day, and I just said out of nowhere that my problem right now is $1,000 dollars. He laughed at me and said if I got $10,000 dollars that instant that my problems would increase. Later, I thought about what he said and realized that the more money, the more responsibilities. There will always be a use for money. It will take financial intelligence to sort out the things that you actually need to use the money for and things you should let go of.

I was lucky I did not get into student debt, but I worked full time, and it took ten years to get my Bachelor's degree. I did not have any other option and looking back. I realize I would not have done it any other way, as I could not decide what I wanted to do after graduating. So, by the time I graduated, I had a lot of experience in the working world.

I remember my first job at Sears. I wanted to be better at what I did and grow within the company. For me, it was always about that. I wanted to make it in life. I had goals! I worked hard to be where I am today and to gain the knowledge I have. We all should continue to grow after college and university. We all need to continue to dream, no matter what trials and tribulations we may face in life.

As I draft this book, it is the time of the COVID-19 pandemic. The unemployment rate is the highest it has ever been since the Great Depression. These are tough times. A lot of businesses have had to close. Some governments could help those who needed help; somehow, people are pulling through. But many people lost their jobs. And, while things are reopening, some businesses cannot find workers. Unemployment benefits have treated some people well, and instead of returning to work and earning money, some people are staying at home. Some are at home doing nothing[21] (and I have never understood how people can allow themselves to become lazy). But others who have been laid off from work because of the pandemic have started their own businesses because that is another exposure that the pandemic made. You

---

[21] Marla Tabaka, "Some see Millennials as lazy and entitled," www.inc.com, Last modified September 7, 2018, https://www.inc.com/marla-tabaka/some-see-millennials-as-lazy-entitled-yet-they-may-be-most-successful-generation-of-our-time.html.

can also venture into a business but ensure you have a prospect for succeeding.

Millennials' insecurity comes from all the competition we have out there, not only with our own age group but with Baby Boomers and Generation Z. So, we have reasons we may have insecurities, but we should not be lazy, especially if we want to be as successful as the Gen X-ers and Gen Z's. You do not necessarily act like you are in competition with anyone. You just need to brace up and deal with your finances, your insecurities, and anything that may drag you down. The competition should be within you. That way, you will not feel so pressured compared to competing with other people, which can be very draining. We need to focus, get committed, and start saving money so we can live the American Dream that has been promised to us—the perfect family, the perfect job, the perfect house. Getting those things has always meant challenging work, but now it is even harder. So, for example, if you want a new house, you will need to jump in and fight for it. Do not just work hard. Work smart, too.

Depending on the state that you live in, the housing market might be crazy, like it is in California, New York, or Florida. So, the idea of owning a house by the time you are 40 may be impossible. If you are just purchasing a home for yourself and your family, it is better late than never. Consider yourself lucky. Globest.com reports that Millennials have the lowest homeownership rates of any other generation.[22]

So, if you want to work smart, an investment in real estate is the best investment. Many multi-millionaires have repeated that this is the way to go; to invest in real estate. Affordability is the biggest hurdle to improving Millennial homeownership, and gaining a down payment is among the top challenges.[23] As long as we work smart and hard, anything is possible. We can achieve our dreams. We can be independent by buying a house (or two). We just need to learn how to do it—and never stop learning.

---

[22] Kelsi Maree Borland, "After 2020, More Millennials Doubt Homeownership," www.globest.com, Last updated February 11, 2021.
http://www.globest.com/2021/02/11/after-2020-more-millennials-doubt-homeownership/?slreturn=20211030180758.
[23] www.globest.com.

What can you take from this chapter?

Start saving, even if it is just $1.00 a day. Pay off your debt, consolidate it, or resolve it. Do not buy everything you want. Do not look at what others are doing. If you cannot pay off your credit card at the end of the month, you cannot afford to spend. Read finance management books or watch YouTube videos instead. You need to educate yourself. Education is power! Figure out what financial plan works for you. Get expert advice. Google Financial Advisors or find some on social media. (They often give free advice.) Never stop growing as an individual. Continue to educate yourself.

Journal Notes

Ask yourself...

1. Do you have debt? What can you do to get rid of it?

_____

_____

_____

2. Do you save?

_____

_____

_____

_____

3. Have you addressed and resolved all your potential problems?

_____

_____

_____

_____

4. Do you continue to learn and grow as an individual?

CHAPTER ELEVEN

_____

_____

_____

_____

Keeping Up
with the Trend

Why is everyone trying to be so trendy? The answer to that question is not far-fetched. There are many reasons why people insist on trends and why they must follow trends. Could it be that we do not look old? Or do we just like being trendy?

A "trend" is what is hip or popular at a certain point in time. We define a trend as going in a general direction or going in a certain way. Trends are reflected in fashion, pop culture, entertainment, and social mores.

Trends are intertwined with society. It is the society that gives trends room for existence. And also, trends differ between societies. What is trending in one society may not be what is trending in another society. Trends have something to do with social acceptance. For the people who create trends, it is for leverage and for recognition. Let us take entertainment, for instance, specifically the music industry. Musicians, when they release a song, put in so much effort to promote it so that it can be the trending song. When it's a trending song, it has gained widespread fanfare, increasing their money on the song. They promote it through different mediums, and people are instrumental in making it a trend. A song will not be regarded as trending if people do not know it or sing it. Now let us see fashion trends. When these fashion designers create their designs, they also promote them through different mediums, of which the commonest is through models. We try to emulate these trends through these models and the other mediums they use. So, you see, trends are created for people to copy. That's just it; trends are mere to be copied. While the creators of the trends get their benefits. Most of the time, it is a financial reward, and next to it will be the fame attached to being the one in trend. That is for the part of the people who create the trends. But for the people who follow trends, let me first state that following trends is not bad. They do it most of the time to feel among others.

I was on social media when I watched an interview with a man who explained why people go for these expensive things like Birkin bags or Jordan shoes. He said when people do not feel they belong to a particular group, they do things that the group members do. In doing that, they already feel like they are a member of the group. So, he said, that's why you will find a young guy saving up to buy Jordan's sneakers. It is not because he needs the sneakers, but he has evaluated a group in the society which he would like to associate himself with, and that sneakers will make him feel like one of them. Also, that's what will explain why someone will actually like a Ford car, but because he wants to show off or belong to a group, he chooses Benz because Benz owners dominate that group.

There are also social media trends. These ones do not often come in material things. It involves copying and uploading what people have done in the form of acts or songs. The social media platform dominating trends now is TikTok. People make videos using the same sound and/or doing the same thing that has been done. As someone that has seen how TikTok is operated, I can say it is not an easy process. You have to go through the recording, the editing, and the final uploading. Through these processes, you must ensure that they are neatly done, in fact, perfect for viewing. If not done that way, you will lose the essence of making the video in the first place, getting people to like and follow you. Basically, TikTok is a battle for social relevance. In fact, that is the whole game of trends. People fight for social relevance through trending activities and materials. To get a perfect video to post on TikTok requires patience and time. You will have to ensure that all irrelevant parts are cropped out, including the shade, the lighting, and so on. You can see that it involves a process as though it is a paid job. Well, some persons, actually, few compared to the greater number, get paid for their videos on the platform. That happens after they have garnered wide social relevance that they now have massive coverage, and people pay them to influence their brands or businesses. The platform is basically for fun.

There are two notable features of trends. First is what I have been discussing since; it is merely a battle for social relevance. Suppose you observe what I have been saying. Almost everyone who follows up on trends does it to either feel accepted or to get recognition in the society where the trend is going on. The second is that trends are not static in nature. A trend may come back later in the future, like the case of palazzo jeans, but it does not stay on trend forever. They have time, and when the time elapses, the trend is over. The trend is replaced by a newer trend. For the trend creators, it is a competition. When their trends get replaced, they try to develop another one or improve on the former one to make it new and present it for the people to follow. Their competitors, who will not relent, come up with their own trends, which will, in turn, replace the former. The cycle keeps going like that. For the people who follow the trends, it creates the picture of a flock of sheep being led by a shepherd. They cannot say exactly where they will go. It is the shepherd who leads. The initial shepherd is replaced with another and another and another, and like that, the sheep are being led to wherever the shepherd wants. That is just a picture of trends and people.

How do we keep up with changing trends? I find it impossible. I have a family and a job and want time for myself. Keeping up with trends requires using four social networking platforms—Facebook, Instagram, Twitter, and TikTok—every day ... even every hour. How can a busy person do that? It is impossible to sacrifice somewhere (unless you are single and your job allows you to spend time on social media). Even staying on top of the news means keeping abreast of social media. Then there are blogs and emails from bloggers; companies that send daily emails with their updates, ideas, and thoughts; online magazines; and ads for products in stores ... How can a person keep up? It is exhausting! As we get older, we must prioritize and be mindful of where our precious time goes.

Personally, I feel trends are for younger people. No, I do not mean that you should not do something trendy if you want to or wear something trendy if you want to. What I mean is that the concern of always being trendy is usually associated with younger people. Following trends means you have to be up and doing about everything that is tagged "trending." Only younger people have so much time to sit before a mirror and make videos all day. The younger people can still go for anything trendy they see because they have lesser responsibility. It is also the younger people who really care about what society thinks of how trendy they are. As an adult, these concerns are not primary. These concerns do not exist for some adults because other concerns have overshadowed them. I find it unrealistic to stay up to date with all the trends. So, I have to ask myself, "Do I even want to be like everyone else?" I do not mind changing a few things here and there, but jumping on the bandwagon, from crop tops to low-rise jeans to never-ending TikTok videos—well, I just cannot do it. I am too old to mimic TikTok videos. I mean, sure, I could if I wanted to, but my focus in life is my quality of life, my family, and what brings me joy. Life is so short! I guess for some people, "life" is the unreal social media and TikTok life; for others, it is about life's true meaning.

I am sure everyone has noticed how, when someone creates a new video on TikTok, everyone makes copycat videos. Why do people waste time copying? I am all for someone who has talent posting TikTok videos of them dancing, singing, or sharing their art. Generation X, it seems, focuses on getting a TikTok video trend going, becoming a blogger, and getting the next big app on the market. When we Millennials were growing up, we focused on careers, education, and moving out of our parent's house. We Millennials think differently from other Generations. We started the trends when we were in our 20s.

Great things are not accomplished by those who yield to trends and fads, and popular opinion.[24]

—JACK KEROUAC

Who sets the trends now? Bloggers? Brands? It used to be that only those with money and power, or demographic groups with large numbers of like-minded individuals, could start a trend. Now anyone can start any trend. All you need is a computer and be social media savvy. Trendsetters need to stay up to date with all that is happening worldwide. Being a blogger is a full-time job!

So, again, do what makes you happy. If social media innovation makes you happy, strive to get into social media, but just understand the reasons you want to do it. Is it important to have lots of followers (for whatever reason), or are you pursuing social media fame because everyone else is doing it? Or are you searching for comfort? If so, what comfort are you looking for on social media? Once you understand the *why* of what you want, it will be easier to achieve your goal. If you are trying to earn money with Instagram, spend more than a few hours a day on it—there is a lot of content to prepare and post. It takes a lot of active Instagram / Facebook / TikTok time to build a strong following, requiring background work. But if you want to be a trendsetter in a changing environment, it is possible!

---

[24] Jack Kerouac, wwwbrainyquotes.com, Access date November 29, 2021, https://www.brainyquote.com/photos_tr/en/j/jackkerouac/119789/jackkerouac1.jpg.

Let us talk about trends. It is not just in social media that things are in flux. In fashion, for example, things are changing faster than most people can keep up with. Just last year, skinny jeans were in style, and a few months ago, the newest trend was baggy wide-legged jeans! I understand that during the COVID-19 virus shutdowns, a few people gained extra pounds (or more than a few), and maybe baggy jeans are perfect for them. But I will not go for baggy jeans. It is not just me. I did some online research (as I always do), and as with all trends, there is a battle of opinions. Some people do not care and will switch with the trend. Not me—I will not give up my skinny jeans. First, I like how they fit. I worked hard for them to look the way they looked. Second, I have a few nice pairs, and I will not let them go or leave them in the closet until the trend is back. Third, I do not consider baggy jeans attractive. I enjoy well-fitted, good-quality clothes. Nothing makes a woman more comfortable than wearing a well-put-together outfit. Others seem to agree. Like me, they are adamant about staying with their skinny jeans.

And this is what I mean. Are we going to follow every fashion trend society presents to us? If everyone shaved their eyebrows off, for example, would you? No, thank you! There is so much out there; the important thing is to evaluate every new trend before "going along." Does it fit your purpose, your lifestyle, and your needs? Make sure that you are thinking about yourself first, not the rest of the trendsetters and their followers. Do not let others influence what you do or what you want to do. As a Millennial, being on this planet for nearly 40 years, you know who you are, what you want, and what you need. Trust yourself and go for it.

In our 40 years, we have gone through a bit. We partied through 2000 when all the computer systems were supposed to crash. On December 21, 2012, we watched in wonder as the Mayan calendar "end of the world" predictions proved false. We have lived through the 9/11 attacks, anthrax threats, multiple hurricanes, President George W. Bush, President Barack Obama, President Donald Trump, the Supreme Court approving same-sex marriages, government shutdown, COVID-19, Bitcoin, and so much more! All of this has happened in the past twenty-two years. We understand the impact of it all, and we are old enough to remember it all. I have learned a lot about myself, who I am as an individual, how I relate to others, and what I am worth. What about you?

Trends are not set for individual happiness or for personal development. Although some personal development coaches try to get people to action by creating trends, they are still not dominating the trend world. The activities that dominate the trending world are vain. I dare to say. I am not against trends in any way. You can do as much as you want to, but at every point, you must ask yourself if it's really what you want. Major people who follow trends do not do it for themselves. They do it for the social acceptance they expect from doing it. If you think a trend can make you happy, do it. Remember, your happiness should be a major consideration. However, if, on the other hand, the trend is not adding value to your life, drop it! Trends are not compulsory. How we see them and how they are presented in society makes them appear as if it is a must-do thing. No, they are not, and I know you know that.

I know there is the pressurizing aspect of trends. You find them so interesting and irresistible. In fact, that is the reason most people are engaged in different trends. They found it irresistible that even if their pocket cannot fund it, they are willing to get it anyway. You should not sacrifice anything for trends; your money, time, etc. These things are precious and should be used on more important things. Trends may give pleasure, but they are temporary in nature. If you ignore and invest in a trend, you will become old-school when another trend surfaces, displacing the one you invested in. You will be behind because you are no longer trending. That is why it is advised that you should not invest so much in trends; they do not last. If a trend makes you happy, do it. I have said it earlier before. Not all trends are vain. At forty, you must know that not all trends are not for you. And the focus of your life should not be battling for social relevance. You know better at this age that those things do not make you happy. Rather, invent your own trends just for yourself. Get the pleasure of doing something for yourself that does not make you feel you are in a battle for relevance. Forty is really not the age when you should be trying out new things that are announced. No, it's not try-outs time. It is time to be perfect! It is time to be solely concentrated on your happiness!

What can you take from this chapter?

Do not follow a trend if it does not suit me. Stop and think. Where should your time be going? Re-evaluate. What matters? What does not?

Journal Notes

_____

_____

_____

_____

_____

_____

_____

_____

_____

_____

_____

_____

_____

_____

_____

_____

_____

Ask yourself...

1. Do you waste your time on social media? Is there something you can do or ways you can spend that same time on social media and make it productive for you?

_____

_____

_____

_____

_____

_____

_____

_____

2. Do you follow trends? If yes, why? If not, why?

_____

_____

_____

_____

_____

_____

_____

_____

CHAPTER TWELVE

Oh, That Guilty Feeling

There are many reasons we feel guilty. Maybe we feel we are not spending enough time with family or too much time with family and not enough with friends. Or, perhaps we need to spend more time at work and less time with family. On the one hand, we feel guilty. On the other, others guilt trip us.

If you feel guilty about your relationship with others, you need to check it. Personal guilt has a positive perspective to it. At least, the way I perceive it is that it is your conscience pushing up the guilt. And if it is your conscience that is at work, it might be right. However, if it is guilt-tripping, the hat is from others and, most times, doesn't matter. Emotional hurts are deeply felt more than physical hurt because it messes up a person's mental stability. Guilt-trip is one way to hurt somebody emotionally. When people guilt-trip someone, they try to push them to a certain level where they become vulnerable. When you get vulnerable, you are likely to bend to the will of the person you are vulnerable to. People guilt-trip to make them get to you and probably use you to the extent they want to use you if you fall for their trap. Yes, a guilt trip is a trap. When people cannot find a way to get you to do what they want or get what they want from you, they find a cunning way to do it. One such way is emotionally tackling you by getting to your head, making you feel like it is your fault. If you are not conscious of this act, you will fall victim. Many people have fallen for it because it is a sneaky way of dealing with people.

The *Merriam-Webster Dictionary* defines "guilt trip" as manipulating someone's behavior by causing them to feel guilt or to have committed a breach of conduct, especially by violating a law that involves a penalty.[25] We get guilt trips almost daily—from strangers, bosses, coworkers, kids, and families. Why? Friends and families try to make us feel guilty for not doing something for them. Others also guilt-trip us for trying to be who we want to be. By age 40, no one in our life should tell us when to do something or why. Although the whole idea of guilt trip is negative, I think it should not all be considered in that light. People may do it deliberately out of the desire to get what they want from you, but you can also consider it to see if there may be truth to their allegations.

---

[25] https://www.merriam-webster.com/dictionary/guilt-trip.

There can only be two reasons why people guilt trip others. First, they are doing it intentionally, meaning they want to see you feel bad. Second, they are not doing it intentionally; they are just doing it unaware of its effect on you. Also, there may be a truth to what the person is alleging you, or it is just a falsity entirely. Whatever the nature is, the reason, or the motive of a guilt trip, you should never fall victim. Earlier in this chapter, I explained how nature would take its course through people. And that means that your life will be scrutinized by many people you come across and those that you already know. Some people will reserve their remarks or comments about your life, but others cannot keep shut about it. They must tell you how they feel you are not doing good in your life. They must tell you how you have risen below expectations at your age. They must tell you how others who are in the same age group are doing better than you. In making that, they guilt trip; they twist the situation and make it about you.

On the other hand, you who would have fallen victim would have sunk their words into your heart, and that is the only thing you have on your mind. It then directs your life, and you live as though you do not know what you are doing. Actually, you do not know what you are doing. You are merely acting on people's opinions, which makes the situation worse because they only give opinions but do not tell you how to go about it. A thirty-five and unmarried woman is a perfect example of this situation. She will suffer a lot of guilt trip due to her unmarried status. People are going to blame her for the condition by alleging various things. They may include accusing her of being too ambitious, being picky, and so on. Meanwhile, the woman had experienced the pains of a failed marriage in her childhood while living with her parents. No one will see this part because they just expect all women to be married at that age. After being guilt-tripped, she has fallen, and now she is rethinking her life and wondering if she had made a mistake. She totally forgets about the reasons why she had made those decisions initially. Then she considered the allegations levied against her and concluded that it must be true for everyone to be saying it. Because of that, she marries a man. She did not enjoy the marriage, and after bearing it for a year, the marriage ended.

By 40, most of us have kids. If we do not, society guilt trips us for not having the family everyone is "expected" to have by 40. Your family tells you that you need to have kids to take care of you when you are old—but they also tell you, "You're getting too old to have kids," or they accuse you of being selfish by focusing on you. But as I said, more women are focusing on their careers and finding themselves—and then, in their 40s, they think of having kids. The "where are your kids?" guilt trips are real.[26] If there is one major effect of a guilt trip, it

---

[26] Jessy Wrigley, "Why do I feel guilty for no reason?" www.myonlinetherapy.com, Last updated March 6, 2020, http://myonlinetherapy.com/why-do-i-feel-guilty-for-no-reason.

is that it affects the happiness of the person concerned. It alters your state of mind on the subject and leaves you wondering whether you have been doing it right all this while.

There are other guilt trips, too. God forbid, for example, we get divorced at 40. Then, we are guilt-tripped about not making our marriages work. What is the solution for guilt-tripping? Do not feel guilty for doing what you want and need to do.

First and foremost, ensure that you are doing what is best for your life. It is very important because you should come first in your life because it is your life. When you are being guilt-tripped, or any allegation is made against you, I would say you should filter it. Do not just debunk it so quickly because they are trying to make you sad in your life. As I said earlier, some do not intend to hurt you when they guilt trip you. They just speak from the reserves of their mind. I keep mentioning this because the lack of intention to hurt may just include truth in the allegation. For instance, as a forty-year-old woman, you are so invested in your career. You love the job and spend so much time at your work. The work also pays you well. Aside from the bills your husband takes care of, you also do some things in the house, like getting your husband and children surprise gifts, taking them out, getting them some things they love, and so on. For a while, your children have been whispering to you that you do not have time for them and that you are so concerned about your work. It has been whispered until the day they reacted seriously to their claims. Earlier, you ignored their claims as demanding too much attention, so you did not let them put you in the trap of a guilt trip. However, looking at the scenario I just created, there is a truth to the claims made by the children. She is not balancing her work and her dedication to her family. Her children especially should have attention from her, and they don't seem to get it. She replaced the attention with the gifts she bought and the shopping she took them to. If she probably was not quick to ignore them and shove their claims aside, she may have realized that her children only needed more of her. Although, she cannot be faulted entirely. She is doing what she loves and caring for her family in the way she can, but you must know that children have added responsibility. When you have kids, you cannot have as much time as you used to have for other affairs. The situation of things will be altered, and your children will have to get some more time. You may not be able to give them the kind of attention they desire, but sufficient is enough. There is a sufficient degree. If you do not do that, your children will seek attention elsewhere, and trust me. They will get it. So, to avoid making hasty decisions that may turn out to be a mistake, it is better to filter the allegations people make against you. If they claim you are lacking in some area, give it a chance to determine if it's true or false before deciding and acting on it. If it's false, trash it like the dirtiest thing you know. If you find that there's a truth to it, it is an opportunity for you to do the right thing. There is the possibility of truth being in the claims and accusations of people because sometimes you may be too busy with your life that you forget to take note. When they make their accusations, don't get busy with action so fast. Chill, think, and deliberate before you then react.

Make yourself happy first. Personally, I have found that if I am happy, everyone around me is happy, too. For example, I used to feel guilty for taking a day off. I felt guilty for leaving the office early to get a bit of sleep after I had been up four times with my young daughter the night before. I felt guilty taking some time to get a massage or to get my hair or nails done. If you are a mom, you know this—mommy guilt is the hardest! Of course, our little ones know how to manipulate us too, how to give us the biggest guilt trip ever. We think we should be at home, playing with them, cooking for them, and doing their laundry instead of doing a bit of self-care. Just so you know, it is NORMAL to want to take a brief break from your everyday routine or to get distracted from real life by enjoying a fun-filled evening out with friends. But when you do, what happens? You feel guilty because you had someone else put them to sleep. Maybe you left the kids with their dad, or their grandparents, or even a babysitter. It is okay. They love them and will take care of them. So, be happy. Have fun and know that your kids get a break from you, and you get a break from them. You both need those breaks every so often. We go through so much with pregnancy, childbirth, and raising our kids. After a couple of years of child-rearing, we change. We can forget who we are.

So many moms I speak to say they were different before they had kids. They had different priorities, and now, with all the responsibilities of motherhood, there is no time for them, their interests and hobbies, or distractions. We think that once we are moms, life changes, that things have to be a certain way. Change is good, but we need to make sure we remember who we are as women first.

Do not feel guilty for doing… what is best for you…[27]
—**DIMPLE KAMBLI**

We are human beings, after all. We get tired. We need distractions. We need space. We need a change of pace. Suppose you are lucky enough to have someone you trust who can help with kids and watch them do it. Use their help while you can. It is not bad to let someone put your kids to sleep once or twice a week or once every two weeks. We do everything for them. We put our time and our energy into them. We deserve that break! So, go out with your friends. Go

---

[27] Dimple Kambli, www.yourquote.com, Access date November 26, 2021, http://www.yourquote.in/dimple-kambli-dxf4/quotes/don-t-feel-guilty-for-doing-what-s-best-you-bcdv7.

to the movies with someone (or even alone) or have a date night with your partner. Do not feel guilty. Be happy!

So, what can you do to not fall into someone's guilt trips?[28] First, establish what you want and need in life. This is a top priority because if you do not know what you want, you will be tossed around by people's opinions. After all, their opinions and suggestions about your life will never end. How many people still get confused about what they should or want to do will surprise you. With all the influences around, being confused is easy. Deep down in your heart, you should know what you want—after all, nearly forty years on this planet have shaped your preferences. Re-establish your priorities. Remember who you are and what you need. Here is how:

- Ask for what you want. Make decisions that lead to getting what you want.

- Build your relationships. Reduce your expectations. What relationships bring you happiness and joy? Focus on those. Let go of relationships that drain you.

- Take responsibility for your feelings. Explore your emotions. Own up to your feelings. Understand why you feel a certain way. Ask yourself why you reacted to something the way you did. Then, change your feelings.

---

[28] Julie de Azevedo Hanks, "5 ways to stop guilt trips and start being assertive," www.newharbinger.com (blog), Last updates February 20, 2017, https://www.newharbinger.com/blog/self-help/5-ways-to-stop-guilt-trips-and-start-being-assertive/.

Let nothing stop you from enjoying your 40s. No one, absolutely no one, should ever make you feel bad for the choices you have made to better your life. If you allow them, you will regret it later. That later, there will be no time to do the things you ought to have done then, although ample time to do that may exist. But you know what they will be doing with their lives? They will live as they want because it's all we ought to do. Don't give regard to all the accusations people make against your life. Filter them and react accordingly. Remember, your next big milestone is fifty!

What can you take from this chapter?

People will make you feel guilty when they need to. You will not fall prey to guilt trips. Know and understand what you want and need. Make sure you are happy first. Let those mommy-guilt feelings go.

Journal Notes

_____

_____

_____

_____

_____

_____

_____

_____

_____

_____

_____

_____

_____

_____

Ask yourself...

1. Do you feel guilty?

_____

_____

_____

_____

_____

2. Do you spend enough time on yourself? If not, why? What can you do to make that happen?

_____

_____

_____

_____

_____

3. Are you happy?

CHAPTER THIRTEEN

_____

_____

_____

_____

_____

_____

Just Be Happy. Be You...

As I get closer to 40, the most important question I ask myself is, "Am I happy?" I have a family, a loving husband, two beautiful daughters, and a wonderful support system. I travel. I spend time with my parents and siblings. Being happy should be easy, right? With all the wisdom and experience I have now, of course, I am happy.

There is an illusion of happiness we have that society creates for us or that other people impose on us. Happiness is a personal thing. However, there can be group happiness that is not primary. Happiness is primarily an individual thing. In this life, the one thing common to our pursuit is happiness. We all struggle to get happy, but why though? Happiness is not given; it is sought. If it was given, we would all have happiness. Most of us think we are happy—at least, we hope we are. But how do we know? Is it easy to be happy? What matters the most for happiness? Are you satisfied with your life? Are you doing what you want? Are you achieving everything you want? Happiness is an individual thing … and it is the most important thing there is. Some people say, "I'm not happy," and then tell you all the reasons happiness evades them. But I have discovered that we must find happiness within ourselves. For the longest time, I thought, "Yes, I'm happy with myself, blah blah blah." It was true. I was happy. But was I 100 percent happy? To be honest, I was maybe halfway there. I thought, "By 40, I should be well-rounded. I should be happy with whatever life throws at me, right?" But then I looked into it and figured out why I was not 100 percent happy. One by one, I looked at situations that upset me. I dissected each situation and found that I always returned to what someone did or said that was not what I wanted. I realized I needed to figure out why I was always looking for a different outcome and reaction. Why did I even have expectations of people or situations?

"Well," I thought, "maybe it was because of how my parents raised me. Maybe what I expected was what I thought was normal." I knew I wanted to change my attitude because getting upset was affecting my happiness. So, each time situations arose that made me unhappy. I did not let things get to me. One event at a time, I let it all go. I told myself, "It does not matter. Why should it? Getting upset does not add to my life; this outcome this other person wants does not take away from my life." Just letting things go made me happy. The more I did this, the happier I got. I stopped expecting things. I realized that in all the aspects of life in which I was not happy, I had been taking things personally and letting them get too close to my heart. I realized I would not find happiness outside of myself. I could only find it inside me.

The search for happiness lies underneath almost all of our actions. If you investigate deeper, you will find that people do a lot of things in their life in the hope that they find happiness. This can account for the complex nature of happiness. Happiness is both simple and complex, depending on the circumstances. Life in itself is a struggle comprising different hurdles and trials. Happiness is the thing that keeps us on our toes and motivates us to the next level. Imagine there was nothing like happiness, and there was life. It's chaotic, right? There will be no gain; you will have to deal with life however you can, and you derive no single pleasure from this world. That's why we have happiness. Happiness is related to other concepts like pleasure, delight, peace, joy, etc. So, whenever we feel these things, we easily say we are happy. The reason why we need to be happy can never be over-flogged; it is very important. Without feeling happy, this life will be unbearable. Finding happiness is the most common remedy for coping with many issues in this life. That is why as a means of escaping so many pains, trauma, or tragedies, people engage in activities they consider will lead to them being happy.

These issues we face in life do not come out as we get older; they start as we step into this world. The gravity of the problem or issue only increases as we get older. As a kid, our needs are not as heightened as adults'. In fact, we had just flimsy needs and issues. The types that ice cream can resolve or those that were getting food or new cloth can resolve. As we get older, our search for happiness increases and in a different context. A teenager likes to party, so she sneaks into a party even though she is forbidden from going because she wants to do it and because her friends are doing it. Our idea of happiness at this age is not well defined because we are only guided by what people tell us., and what we see in society. We try out different things because of the opinion that we have that such can make you happy. Then we progress, grow older, and we know more. If at all, at this age, you know what makes you happy. That is one thing that has been emphasized the most in this book at this age -age forty- you already know what you want. That is why they say life begins at forty because your previous years have only been tryouts. You have been engaging in different activities, meeting people, and testing yourself all the way, and at this point, you now know what it is you want.

Happiness is tied to our wants and not necessarily needs. Needs sometimes are prompted by what we see from others and not what we truly want for ourselves. However, our wants will always determine how happy we will be. As a young person, you have not really discovered your wants. That is why you could do anything and say you were happy because even you did not know if you were happy. As a forty-year-old, your wants should be defined, and only then will you be able to derive true happiness because the satisfaction of your wants leads to your happiness. That is why there is no true happiness in doing what people tell you to do because it is just that; what they want you to do! It is what you want that determines your happiness. From your experience, you have lived according to how you were asked to. You probably chose a course your parents wanted you to choose. You probably lived in a manner your parents thought was best. That should not be the order of your life anymore. What you want is what you should do. It is your life; you should not live it fulfilling the wants of others. Whatever other people say is what they want, although, sometimes, what they want may align with what you want. Still, learn to discard what people want for your life. It will make them happy, yes. But is that what you want to do with your life? Making other people happy? It is your life, and everybody got theirs. It is excusable as a young person that you live your life doing what people want or think you should want. It is excusable because you are just young and inexperienced. But it is not justifiable as an adult that you are to prioritize what people say over what you say. Your needs and wants should overrule what other persons say at all times, principally because it is your own happiness you seek for. Every single person has the power to make themselves happy. You are not responsible for making another person's happiness the purpose of your life. And you should never let them convince you otherwise because they will attempt to.

The only thing that will make you happy is being happy with who you are.[29]
—GOLDIE HAWN

I started researching how to find happiness within. I realized that the things that stop us from finding our inner happiness are all the pressures out there—all the things I mentioned before—social media and social expectations. We compare our happiness with material things, with someone else having better things, with someone doing better than us. We see the greener grass and let ours turn yellow. I used to compare myself to others. It is so easy to fall into this game. If you are lucky, you are there only to take what you need from social media ... and from that perspective, it has a lot to offer. For everyone else—social media can be a trap. Like a game you get into and cannot stop playing.

We have talked about this before, but it bears repeating here. With social media being the powerhouse of our lives,

---

[29] Goldie Hawn, "Goldie Hawn Quotes," www.brainyquotes.com, Access date July 12, 2021, https://www.brainyquote.com/quotes/goldie_hawn_387167.

how easy is it to be yourself? And what does it mean to be yourself? From an early age, we are told who we need to be. People advise us to do this and not do that, to like this and not like that. They want us to like certain foods, dislike certain drinks, like certain people, and dislike certain TV shows. In some ways, social media is the biggest culprit for making us want to fit in—to be someone we are not. To be yourself means to be true to your core identity instead of faking a different one because you think it will be attractive to others. Only a few of us are true to ourselves. So many of us try to be someone else.

As I said earlier, happiness is rooted in our wants. Our wants are necessitated by who we are. There was so much tossing when we were younger because we did not know who we really were and so we didn't know our wants then it was dictated to us. Happiness lies in discovery. Discover who you are, what kind of personality you have, and what kind of things you like. It is on these discoveries that your wants will be built. At forty, you should have made your discoveries. That is why you will have confidence against any opposition from anybody. You know for sure what you are, and no one needs to tell you who you are and how to live your life. Only when you have discovered who you are and live your life according to who you have discovered can you truly be happy. It may seem like happiness, but if you live according to what people say, it will come crumbling on you one day. That will be the day you realize that you have not been living your life but the life of others, and you have wasted so much time doing what they said, pleasing them, and making them happy.

You, yes, you. You need to prioritize your happiness. Find you and live you beautifully. When people talk against it, ignore them, and see the compromise eventually. When you do as people say, it means they are the commander of your life, and it is not supposed to be so because we all have our lives to live and command.

I am almost 40. I know who I am, what I like, and what I dislike. Before I turned 40, I wanted to take each thought in my mind and evaluate it. Was it mine? Or was it my parents,' siblings, grandparents, teachers, friends, social media, and the rest of the world? I had to evaluate all my expectations, too. I found out I wanted way more out of my life. I looked at all I had achieved and wanted to do more. Life is short. It is too short not to be authentic about everything in your life—about what you think, what you want out of life, and who your friends are.

We all have friends. We care about them, and they care about us. But do they? Do we? How many of our friends care about us, and how many are there just for show? In my 20s and early 30s, I thought everyone was my friend and would be there for me no matter what. I mean, we partied together three nights out of seven, right? Why wouldn't they be there for me if I fell? Guess what? All those people's opinions I cared about because I thought they were my besties disappeared! They moved on with their lives, with their priorities, their agendas. And that is okay. But I realized I had wasted my time worrying about what they thought of me. I was not truly myself when I was with them. I tried to be like them. I thought we shared the same opinions, interests, and values. Now they are gone. Sure, we check in every so often with each other, but that is about it. It was fun, but I would not have wasted my time if I could have done it another way. I would have focused on growing and learning more about myself.

If I could tell my younger self one thing, it would be, "Don't waste your time trying to fit in with others." I followed all the trends with my cool friends. Why? Because I did not know myself back then. I did not realize that as you grow, everything around you changes, and you also have to change. Remember how, ten years ago, you loved partying until 3:00 a.m.? You probably do not like it now. Now, you prefer staying at home. So, grow your knowledge. Learn something and keep changing!

If I could do it over again, I would spend more time learning things and not wasting my time and money on partying. Those days are gone for me, so I will be happy if anyone else can learn from my experience. Invest in yourself first, then follow the trends if you want to. Do not get dragged into living the 9:00 – 5:00 life. Start your own business if you have always wanted to do one. Be free. When you are almost

40 and reflect on your life, only doing what you want and being yourself will make you happy.

We complicate ourselves. We wake up and run our lives by standards set by others. We think that to fit in, we have to follow others' trends. If we do not, we think people will ask, "What on earth is wrong with you?" There are quite a few articles and blogs out there on how you should start your day, how you should behave, how you should be, how to be this, that, or the other thing. There are too many expectations! So, set your own standards. Do not let anyone tell you how to be or who you need to be!

Take a little time to get to know yourself. Accept your past. Understand that your parents did all they could for you. The root of it all (good or bad) started there. Your upbringing formed your personality. If you do not like who you are, change. Find out about your past and how it affects the person you have become. For example, we know little about our grandparents and great-grandparents, what they were like, and what they did. Talk to whomever you still have in your family. Find out about their past and discover what they were told about their parents' past. There are different connections in their pasts that can help you understand more about yourself.

Figure out what your standards are. Know your pluses and minuses. Learn to filter, process, and reject all unwanted and unneeded stuff. Find your way. You do not want to live a life of regret because that is what you get when you live other people's lives. You begin to have a lot of "had I known" moments. It is sad because you will wish you could go back in time, and unfortunately, you cannot go back in time. Fortunately, you know what you can do now. You can begin to live your life now. It's not even late to start: life begins at forty. Take nothing to heart. Never stop reaching for more. That does not mean you shouldn't be content; that is not what I am saying! Be content with what you have—your car, where you live, and your job. Never stop learning. Not just learning about yourself but learning about the world around you. This is how you grow as an individual. We cannot just go to college or university and say, "That is enough. I have an excellent job, and I am done with learning." That is so wrong! Never stop. That is what will make you happy.

There are many ways to learn to be happy every day, from keeping a gratitude journal to repeating inspirational quotes, joining spiritual groups, and setting and meeting goals. So, start that journal, tack affirmations up around your house, join that group you have been meaning to join, and set your goals. Once you have reached a goal, look around. Set another one. It is so rewarding to set goals, achieve them, and then set more, bigger, and better ones! You learn so much about who you are when you continue to strive to grow. Again, this is not about acquiring Chanel bags, BMWs, and Jimmy Choo shoes. There are so many meaningful goals you can set. Just start with one. Set daily, weekly, monthly, and yearly goals. Achieving them is the best feeling. You will learn something about yourself that you may have never known. You will get inspired!

Like everyone else, I was looking for inspiration in my life. I hoped to find someone to help me improve my mood and boost my happiness level. You know—that person who always has a smile on their face and who just makes your day. I realized I was that person. I had to cheer myself up. Once you realize you are that person, it is hard to bring you down. Do you know what helped lift my spirits? Writing a gratitude journal every night right before bed.

I prepare the kids for bed, and after they sleep, I take fifteen minutes and reflect on my day. I write at least seven things about myself that I am grateful for and record seven things about others I am grateful for. When I started this habit, it was a struggle to write seven things. But I discovered that the more I wrote, the more things I discovered I was grateful for.

It also helped me tremendously to do some soul-searching about how I could be a better person. I asked myself, "What can help me be happier?" I followed influencers that lifted me up and removed all those "nagging nannies" from my daily encounter list. I read uplifting books. I went on hikes. I spent time alone to connect with myself. I accepted the facts of my life. I remembered the past—the mistakes I had made, my happy moments, my regrets. I separated people around me into two groups: those who make me happy and those who do not make me happy. I moved away from those who do not make me happy and socialized more with those who make me happy.

So, if you want to be happy, find yourself. Discover your emotions and your abilities. Always strive for more knowledge. This is how you continue to grow and develop into a better and happier you. Even people will tell you to be happy, and they will be the ones telling you how to be happy. Yes, they can tell you to be happy but can't tell you how. How to be happy is all in your hands. Your life actually determines your happiness. That is why you should find your life and live your life in the manner that you should dictate for yourself. There is no end to discoveries. The fact that you have fully discovered yourself. Life is an adventure; it keeps going as the adventure continues. Your quest to find more ways to happiness continues. Do not put an end to it, and don't let people get to you that you should rest because it is not for your age. Happiness is not limited by age. Just as there were different ways you could find happiness when you were younger, so it is now. The only difference that exists is the substance of your happiness. It is a myth that happiness decreases when you get older. As long as life continues, there will always be different ways and opportunities to make yourself happy irrespective of your age. Just always stay happy because it is at least the one superpower you've got.

What can you take from this chapter?

Do not change yourself. Learn to accept failures in your life, let them go, and make sure to learn lessons from them. Find what brings you joy and happiness, and be happy. Find a job that fulfills you every day. Exercise.

Journal Notes

_____

_____

_____

_____

_____

_____

_____

_____

_____

_____

_____

_____

_____

_____

_____

_____

_____

Ask yourself...

1. Are you content and happy, or are you living someone else's life?

    _____

    _____

    _____

    _____

2. Do you do what makes you happy? Something that fulfills you every day?

    _____

    _____

    _____

    _____

    _____

3. Do you have a hobby? What is it? How does it make you happy, and why?

    _____

    _____

    _____

    _____

    _____

    _____

CHAPTER FOURTEEN

Explore

Forty is where life begins been the crux of our discussion since. If you have not invested in exploring, this is when you can do it. Get busy exploring options for your happiness. Many people do a lot of exploration because of the fear of missing out (FOMO). It's not a good feeling because it's a regret-like feeling. Although it is not associated with being forty, only a few people actually feel that way. A lot of people can live well without fearing that they are missing out on other things. I am not asking you to develop the fear of missing out, but you can treat your forties that way. There are many things you are missing out on, so you should explore them. For me, there is no restriction to the exploration.

There is a dominant belief in society that the younger days were more interesting, and that is because of the many explorations we did carefree and carefully. And there is also the belief that as you get older, your explorations decrease because you ought to be more serious about life. I would like you to debunk it because nobody wrote the constitution of life. Even assuming there was, it would be an injustice to restrict adventures or explorations to younger people. As long as you know what you are doing, you should not be disallowed from doing what you want to do. Because of how these beliefs get to us, there are many things we leave undone, untouched sometimes, which tend to bring us happiness.

Many books exist on what you should and should not do before you die. None of us know when we are going to go and when we will die. But as with anything else in life, it is important to live life by experiencing life through living through an experience. Do not let the fear of death grapple you and make you feel sad. It is true that you must die, but you must make every day worth it. Let each day count, so you will know that you lived. I once saw a quote from Oscar Wilde that said, "many exist but do not live." Does it sound confusing? Because you feel to exist is to have lived, right? Well, there is a difference between them. Although for you to have lived means you existed. But you may exist and not live. Those who only exist are the people who never had the time to discover their life and live according to the discovery. They probably spend the whole of their lives being tossed to different corners by people's opinions until they end up in a hole that no one can escape. However, those who existed and lived are the people that made the most out of their lives. They engaged in activities that yielded their happiness and probably shared the impact with people.

When I talked about happiness in the previous chapters, I mentioned that you should make discoveries and that there is no end to the discoveries you make about your life. There is a new thing to learn as each day passes. As vast as this world is, so are the opportunities vast. Some of you, you just cannot tell if you like something or not, and that is because you have never tapped it. The things you can say you love and dislike or hate, you can say that about them because you have experienced them. Experience new things. Open your mind to new activities. This is all to ensure sure happiness. There is no limit to your findings. Your only limitation is you, and there is no word for over-happiness. No one measures happiness somewhere and says you are too happy; happy is happy. Explore! Explore! You have ideas in your head before, but the ideas are always pushed away by the thought of what people will say. No, don't give that a chance. Why should you worry about what people will say about your own life? Like, it is your life. At least, I emphasized one thing in one of the previous chapters; people will always talk! Whether you are having fun, they will say you are too old for it. When you are not having fun, they will say you are boring. Is it still this same set of people who always have different things to say that you worry about what they will say? Any idea you wish to try out, try it without giving first thought to what others will say. Instead, your considerations should be, "will I like it?" "I would love to try it." There are many – I say many confidently because this life has so many things in it – opportunities out there for you to try.

I have always found travel a wonderful source of knowledge. We learn so much about life and the world out there when we travel. And do not just stick to one part of the world. Experiencing diverse cultures is extremely important. Everywhere I traveled, I was able to communicate. Either it was that I found English speakers, or I learned a thing or two about their native language. But almost everyone speaks at least a little bit of English around the world, making traveling so much easier. One big piece of advice I have for anyone is to travel. Take at least one trip a year. Go somewhere new. Take a friend if you have no spouse or kids. Enjoy other cultures. Enjoy foods. Enjoy everything about traveling.

One other thing to do if you have not done it yet is to try a different profession. I know it may sound weird, but have you ever imagined being someone else other than, let us say, an accountant, medical biller, doctor, or attorney? Have you ever thought or dreamt about being someone else? As kids, we dream of being someone, try to remember who we wanted to be as a kid, and explore that option. If you do not remember what you wanted to be when you grew up, see what sounds really promising. Try it. You will be surprised. That may be something that will make you so much happier.

Another wonderful thing to do if you have not done it yet is to make a difference in someone's life. Volunteer, teach someone how to read, train someone, mentor someone. The list is endless. Do something that will change someone's life. It will feel like the greatest achievement in your life. How about building a well in a country that cannot afford it? It really doesn't cost so much! How about paying $50 a month and helping someone get educated in another country? The possibilities are really endless. Once you do something like that, you will be inspired to help more and inspire others to do the same. Not only that, but you will feel an amazing sense of accomplishment and have a legacy in people's minds. Whether you care about how you will be remembered or not, impacting someone's life is always remembered. If it is something you can do, try to do it. It is not because of what people will say about you but about how you are projecting your life onto someone. It is one of the best ways to live, knowing that someone in the world is a beneficiary of your impact. It does not have to be a large community or a group of persons. Just one person is enough. You don't need the whole world or many people before you can impact.

Another one to try is meditation. You probably have heard that multiple times. But to all honestly, it brings more than just a piece to you and your life. It teaches you how to respond to the world and people around you, it teaches you how to act around people, and most importantly, it helps you understand limitless things in your life. Meditation is exceptionally good for relaxing, connecting with yourself, and understanding yourself. There are so many benefits to meditation. Try it, do not give us one try. Keep doing it. You will get to enjoy the benefits that meditation has to offer. You can meditate through yoga. I am not saying this to follow a popular opinion, but speaking from experience: yoga is very relaxing, and you never know because you have not tried it.

Learn a new hobby. When we start something new, we shift our focus to that something new, from someone old and unwanted. Like unwanted memories and worries, they go away and do not seem so important anymore when you are so interested in going to play golf. If a new hobby you tried is not quite what you thought, move on to the next. Your brain needs to be occupied with better thoughts and ideas than in the past. We all know we cannot change the past; we can make a change in our future. If you have not read books before or have not ventured into different genres, try it now. You may find that you like reading. If you don't do sporting activities before, you may find that it is something you love and never want to stop. You can even learn new skills. Yes, even that has no age limitation.

Create a wish list or bucket list. Cross one at a time! You may find a bucket list frivolous or childish but do it. After all, you want to do things that make you feel young, right? A bucket or wish list should be a compendium of things you want to try. Are they bizarre? Include it. Are they childish? Include it. Don't you think it is possible? Include it. Do not worry about the possibility of ticking all the items on your bucket list. There can only be two end results: you either tick it or leave it unticked. Whatever the result, you cannot predict, so include it and try it out. Do not wait till tomorrow to create a list. Creating a list is the first step toward your wish! Create, plan, and execute! Do it with your kids, spouse, or friend to make it more fun. Or just do it and be yourself. Do not wait for anyone. If you wait for someone to decide or agree, that may not happen. Just do it.

Face your life with no limitations or restrictions. Think about the things you had once thought about doing, do them now. In all, ensuring that they are safe and trying out is not the most important thing, but it is that it should make you happy. If you know within yourself that you will not like to try it out or that it can never make you happy, then there is no need to try it out. But if it's something you have no idea of its effect on your happiness, you can try it out. The popular saying is that "there is no harm in trying."

You should not let the thought about your age prevent you from exploring. You are not old for exploring or adventures. You are merely creating memories you would love to reflect on in your next milestones. Imagine having a lot to talk about when you are older. Apart from the fact that people will see you as interesting and adventurous, you will also feel accomplished. Nothing can beat the feeling of knowing you did something that made you happy. You are creating memories that no one can take from you. Think about it, if you live through your forties, not worrying about people's opinions but you kept yourself busy by discovering yourself and exploring many opportunities, you will almost forget that you are forty. When people ask about your age, you will probably realize, "Oh, I am forty!"

Yes, explore and keep exploring until you cannot explore anymore. The truth is that if death does not come, there will be a time when you will not be able to do any of these things. What you will be living on are the memories you are creating now.

What can you take from this chapter?

Try something new, do something you have never done, and don't have to be afraid.

Journal Notes

_____

_____

_____

_____

_____

_____

_____

_____

_____

_____

_____

_____

_____

_____

_____

_____

Ask yourself...

1. What did I always want to try but never did for whatever reason?

   _____

   _____

   _____

2. What do I need to do to try to do #1?

   _____

   _____

   _____

   _____

3. What can I do to make a difference in someone else's life?

   _____

   _____

   _____

   _____

4. What am I scared of, if anything?

   _____

   _____

   _____

   _____

CHAPTER FIFTEEN

Oh, How We All Wish
We Could Stay Young Forever

We will all go through moments in our lives when we wish we could stay young forever. Some of us will long repeat the best times of our lives. Others will yearn to return to their best looks, their best energy, and their best health. It will be different for everyone. I dare to say that we have these feelings because of the belief that life is best lived before thirty. Besides that, I know that life before forty was not as restrictive as forty because of the changes that occur to the body, specifically.

We fear getting old, but most of us do not speak about it. We hear this sentiment more from older generations—Baby Boomers, the Silent Generation, and the Greatest Generation—but we do not hear it much from those in their

40s. But none of us can turn back time. We will not live forever; our time is limited. Even if we are lucky enough to live to eighty, ninety, or 100 years of age, we are still limited. Our resources are depleted, our health declines, our abilities diminish, and our bodies age with time.

We should rather fix our minds and concentrate on the things that will move us forward. There is a woman, Agnes. Agnes was as beautiful as the morning star in her twenties. She knew it, and people told her a lot. She enjoyed the attention that came from being a very beautiful lady. The boys and even girls are all over her. She gets invites to all parties. People always gave her first-class treatment. They always liked to associate with her because, apart from being so beautiful, she was always full of life. Life went on, and Agnes got older. She gets a modeling job that pays her so well. She got older and separated from almost all her childhood, teenage, and university friends. One day, Agnes checked in at work and met with the shock of her life. The agency found another model to replace Agnes because she was no longer fit for that particular role. They didn't lay her off. They only wanted her to move to another category. Agnes goes home and checks herself and sees that she is getting old, which has affected the job she loves so much. She is just 37. Agnes refused to take the role in the new category and left the agency. She began searching for a similar job. It took her a while before she found something remote, which she settled for eventually because she was tired.

Agnes started drifting away from people because she felt her life had been taken from her. She also noticed she did not get the attention she used to get from people. She never considered the reason behind that, which is that the other people have moved on with their lives, and things are not the way they used to be. She spent long hours thinking that her life had diminished. Agnes spent the rest of her next 12 years dealing with not being the way she used to be in her twenties and early thirties. It was until Agnes met a woman who opened her eyes to many truths and realities that she finally understood her life and started living at 49.

One reason why Agnes' life turned out that way was because of her expectation to remain the same forever. It is a great illusion to want to remain young forever. Yes, I know it is desirable, but it is never possible. It has never happened to anyone, and it will never happen to anyone. It is quite absurd to want to remain young for life. Change is constant and happens to everyone, even without their will. Instead of accepting the change in her life, Agnes dwelt for a long time in her past. Did you notice what happened to her as a result of that? She didn't live her forties. She was busy trying to return to the past that could not be revisited and missed her forties. She probably would have missed her fifties if not for the assistance of the older woman. There is the possibility that Agnes could have loved the new role at her place of work, but she hindered that possibility by never checking it out. It was more like she was obsessed with her past.

I know we loved our younger selves, the looks, energy, and spirits. But life does not end at forty. Life ends when it ends literally. Until then, we ought to keep living.

f you try to stay young forever, you do not really live.[30]
—ELIZABETH MITCHELL

Acceptance is a whole chapter on its own in this book, and I guess you can see the reason why. It is very important that you accept some things and embrace them that way. It is for the progress of your life. If you never learn to accept, you will be drawn back by the things you do not want to accept. You have done much at your younger age, and there is also much to do now that you are older. Trying to stay young forever for what reason, exactly? It is more like being stuck in a place, and when you are stuck, you don't know anything apart from what surrounds the place you are stuck in. Have you tried to live forty the way you are? No, you haven't, and if you haven't, it means you don't even know how interesting it will get.

---

[30] Elizabeth Mitchell, www.enquoted.com, Access date December 5, 2021, https://www.enquoted.com/elizabeth-mitchell--if-you-try-to-stay-young-forever-you-don-t-really-live-quote.html.

Surprisingly, you may love it more than in your younger days. There is that possibility, and you should not rule it out with your obsession with being younger.

There is a sizable number of wise quotes, statements, and reminders from older people that advise us to slow down and appreciate life, enjoy every day, and live without waiting for tomorrow. I do that now—but I took every day of my 20s and 30s for granted! I realize now that when I am fifty-five, I do not want to look back fifteen years and realize what I had that I did not celebrate. When I am sixty-five, I do not want to wake up one morning and realize I did not appreciate *myself* enough. So many sixty-, seventy-, eighty-, and ninety-year-olds wish they could turn back time and go back to being 30 or 40 again.

Think about this: you probably want to be young again because of the things you did, right? You find them so memorable, interesting, daring, or challenging. And you would love to go back to relive those moments. Then why not now? Create those memories again to the extent that you can so that when you are older, you will want to go back to being forty.

How many of us can be honest and tell ourselves that we appreciate who we are and who we have become right here and right now? We have all learned so many lessons and gone through so many stressors, and amid it all, it has been hard to appreciate ourselves. I have always thought, "Well, I have a lifetime. I'll get around to it." But here I am, almost 40. I hope I have another 40. And whatever number I get to live to, I want to make sure I appreciate myself and love myself for who I am today, every day, in every moment.

Love yourself. No one can love you more than you can, so start doing it right now. What does it take for you to love and appreciate yourself? Work on being in love with you. Accept who you are, love yourself for who you are, and it will feel like a breath of fresh air because you have dealt with the major hindrance to living in your forties. You will never be the way you were before, and worrying about something like that is a complete waste of time. Worry about loving yourself.

You have not lived your best life yet until you say so. Let every day of your forties be worth it. Live it in a way that you will have something inspiring and memorable to tell others. Respect yourself. Admire yourself. Forgive yourself. Start today. *Do that.*

To fall in love with yourself is the first secret to happiness.[31]
—ROBERT MORLEY

[31] Robert Morley, www.quotefancy.com, Access date December 10, 2021, https://quotefancy.com/quote/1596484/Robert-Morley-To-fall-in-love-with-yourself-is-the-first-secret-to-happiness.

WHAT CAN I TAKE FROM THIS BOOK?

1. It is okay to feel different when your birthday comes. A lot of things have changed in the past year. No one should stay the same. You need to continue to change for the better.

2. The older you get, the more confident you get.

3. You know what you want in life. It is okay to feel emotional about getting older.

4. You need to listen to your body and mind.

5. If something bothers you, you must pay attention and figure it out. You will not just ignore it.

6. You will make the changes you wish to see, even if it is one step at a time.

7. Do not stay quiet. You should talk to someone of a similar age. Others are probably feeling the same way you do about the challenges of aging.

8. Remind yourself of all the experiences you have had.

9. Forgive yourself for any mistakes. We all make mistakes. Fix mistakes and apologize if you can.

10. Take time for yourself every day. Take a few hours, one hour, or a few minutes, and reconnect with yourself. You will get a lot of answers.

11. Remember, age is just a number. That number has nothing to do with your goals, dreams, or achievements.

12. Remind yourself (every day if you must) that age is just a number. Set a reminder on your phone, on a Post-it® note next to your dresser, or somewhere you will see it first thing every morning.

13. Remind yourself whatever you have to remind yourself every morning or every day.

14. No one should tell you that you are too old. You can do whatever you want at whatever age you want.

15. The most important thing is how I feel, and not what my date of birth says.

16. Do not lie about your age. Why? Because you would be lying to yourself first. Lying is not healthy. It will not get you anywhere. People will judge you no matter what you do.

17. Other people's opinions do not matter. They are not living your life; you are living your life.

18. Accept changes as challenges. You can do it!

19. Make yourself happy first. Then you can help and support others in finding their happiness.

20. Appreciate yourself now, not in ten years. If you do not, you will regret it.

21. Do not compare yourself to others. Have fun!

22. Be proud of your age.

23. Love your age. It is evidence of your experience and your expertise.

24. Love yourself. Practice self-love. There are many ways to get there. Research and find a way that works for you.

25. We all will feel "our age" eventually.

26. Do your routine physicals every year. You have nothing to lose, and you may prevent something that can be bigger than you want.

27. Accept changes and adapt to them.

28. Be happy.

29. Be grateful.

30. Experiment, find your way to accept the changes, and work with them.

31. You are not alone; You are not going crazy.

32. Enjoy every moment of your life; live each day.

33. Do not let fear control you or your life.

34. Appreciate those who matter in your life.

35. Start saving, even if it is just $1.00 a day.

36. Pay off your debt, consolidate it, or resolve it.

37. Do not buy everything you want.

38. Do not look at what others are doing. If you cannot pay off your credit card at the end of the month, you cannot afford to spend.

39. Read finance management books or watch YouTube videos instead. You need to educate yourself. Education is power!

40. Figure out what financial plan works for you. Get expert advice. Google Financial Advisors or find some on social media. (They often give free advice.)

41. Never stop growing as an individual. Continue to educate yourself.

42. Do not follow a trend if it does not suit me.

43. Stop and think. Where should your time be going? Re-evaluate. What matters? What does not?

44. People will make you feel guilty when they need to.

45. You will not fall prey to guilt trips.

46. Know and understand what you want and need.

47. Make sure you are happy first.

48. Let those mommy-guilt feelings go.

49. Do not change yourself for others.

50. Learn to accept failures in your life, let them go, and make sure to learn lessons from them.

51. Find what brings you joy and happiness, and be happy.

52. Find a job that fulfills you every day.

53. Exercise.

54. Try something new, do something you have never done, and don't be afraid.

55. Be Happy. Life is short.

Journal Notes

PERFECT 40!

Appendix – Worksheets

PERFECT 40!

REFERENCES

Adesina, Precious. "Women Lying About Their Age Is Getting Old."
www.refinery29.com. Last updated December 3, 2018.
http://www.refinery29.com/en-gb/why-women-lie-about-their-age.

Batten, Joseph. www.picturequotes.com. Access date November 26,
2021. http://www.picturequotes.com/our-strengths-are-our-tools-our-personal-reality-our-weaknesses-are-only-what-we-are-not-quote-198452.

Berry, William. "Acceptance: It Isn't what you think."
www.psychologytoday.com. Last updated June 27, 2015.
https://www.psychologytoday.com/us/blog/the-second-noble-truth/201506/acceptance-it-isnt-what-you-think.

Borland, Kelsi Maree. "After 2020, More Millennials Doubt
Homeownership." www.globest.com. Last updated February 11,
2021. http://www.globest.com/2021/02/11/after-2020-more-millennials-doubt-homeownership/?slreturn=20211030180758.

Bursten, Ketura. "7 Serious problems Millennials face today."
www.therapyinbeverlyhills.com (blog). Access date December

10, 2021. https://www.therapyinbeverlyhills.com/7-serious-problems-millennials-face-today/.

Chanel, Coco. www.azquotes.com. Access date December 5, 2021. https://www.azquotes.com/quote/1358434.

Council of Economic Advisers, The. "15 Economic Facts About Millennials." White House. Last updated October 2014. https://obamawhitehouse.archives.gov/sites/default/files/docs/millennials_report.pdf.

de Azevedo Hanks, Julie. "5 ways to stop guilt trips and start being assertive." www.newharbinger.com. Last updated February 20, 2017. https://www.newharbinger.com/blog/self-help/5-ways-to-stop-guilt-trips-and-start-being-assertive/.

Einstein, Albert. www.brainyquotes.com. Access date December 5, 2021. http://www.brainyquote.com/quotes/albert_einstein_125368.

Ellis-Bextor, Sophie. www.brainyquotes.com. Access date December 10, 2021. https://www.brainyquote.com/quotes/sophie_ellisbextor_428884.

Ford, Henry. www.brainyquote.com. Access date November 29, 2021. http://www.brainyquote.com/quotes/henry_ford_133753.

Frazee, Gretchen. "Millennials report more stress than older Americans during Pandemic." www.pbs.org. Last modified August 8, 2020. https://www.pbs.org/newshour/health/millennials-report-more-stress-than-older-americans-during-pandemic.

Hanson, Melanie. "College Graduation Statistics."
www.educationdata.com. Last Modified August 9, 2021.
https://educationdata.org/number-of-college-graduates.

Hawn, Goldie. "Goldie Hawn Quotes." www.brainyquotes.com.
Access date July 12, 2021.
https://www.brainyquote.com/quotes/goldie_hawn_387167.

Hepburn, Audrey. www.quotefancy.com. Access date November 29,
2021. http://quotefancy.com/quote/3886/Audrey-Hepburn-
The-beauty-of-a-woman-is-not-in-a-facial-mode-but-the-true-
beauty-in-a.

Jung, Carl. www.goodreads.com. Access date December 5, 2021.
http://www.goodreads.com/quotes/4483092-life-really-does-
begin-at-forty-up-until-then-you.

Kambli, Dimple. www.yourquote.com. Access date November 26,
2021. http://www.yourquote.in/dimple-kambli-
dxf4/quotes/don-t-feel-guilty-for-doing-what-s-best-you-bcdv7.

Kerouac, Jack. www.brainyquotes.com. Access date November 29,
2021.
https://www.brainyquote.com/photos_tr/en/j/jackkerouac/11
9789/jackkerouac1.jpg.

Livingston, Gretchen. "They're waiting longer, but U.S. Women
today are more likely to have children than a decade ago."
www.pewresearch.com. Last updated January 18, 2018.
https://www.pewresearch.org/social-
trends/2018/01/18/theyre-waiting-longer-but-u-s-women-
today-more-likely-to-have-children-than-a-decade-ago/.

Mandela, Nelson.
https://www.pinterest.com/pin/543668986245093192.

Mitchell, Elizabeth. www.enquoted.com. Access date December 5, 2021. https://www.enquoted.com/elizabeth-mitchell--if-you-try-to-stay-young-forever-you-don-t-really-live-quote.html.

Morley, Robert. www.quotefancy.com. Access date December 10, 2021. https://quotefancy.com/quote/1596484/Robert-Morley-To-fall-in-love-with-yourself-is-the-first-secret-to-happiness.

Rowling, J. K. www.goodreads.com. Access date December 5, 2021. http://www.goodreads.com/quotes/67454-understanding-is-the-first-step-to-acceptance-and-only-with.

Salmonson, Karen. "7 aging quotes: inspiring reminders to feel happy about getting older." www.notsalmon.com (blog). https://www.notsalmon.com/2018/11/10/aging-quotes-inspiring/. Access date December 1, 2021.

Schilling, Deb. "You're Turning 40-Embracing Both Physical and Emotional Changes at this Milestone Birthday." www.mankatoclinic.com. Last updated February 9, 2015. http://www.mankatoclinic.com/youre-turning-40.

Smith, Brad. www.picturequotes.com. Access date November 29, 2021. http://www.picturequotes.com/millennials-and-the-generations-that-follow-are-shaping-technology-this-generation-has-grown-up-quote-1008269.

Tabaka, Marla. "Some see Millennials as lazy and entitled." www.inc.com. Last modified September 7, 2018. https://www.inc.com/marla-tabaka/some-see-millennials-as-lazy-entitled-yet-they-may-be-most-successful-generation-of-our-time.html.

Wrigley, Jessy. "Why do I feel guilty for no reason?" www.myonlinetherapy.com. Last updated March 6, 2020. http://myonlinetherapy.com/why-do-i-feel-guilty-for-no-reason.

URLs

acog.org. https://www.acog.org/womens-health/faqs/having-a-baby-after-age-35-how-aging-affects-fertility-and-pregnancy#.

Merriam-Webster. https://www.merriam-webster.com/dictionary/guilt-trip.

https://www.choosingtherapy.com/midlife-crisis-in-men/

Reading List

Hills, Maisie. *Perimenopause Power*. ISBN: 978-1472978868.

Lee, John R., MD. *What Your Doctor May Not Tell You About Premenopause: Balance Your Hormones and Your Life from Thirty to Fifty*. ISBN: 978-0446673808.

Mead, Lindsey. *On Being 40 (ish)*. ISBN: 978-1501172120.

Sellers, Ronnie, ed. *40 Things to Do When You Turn 40*. ISBN: 978-1569069868.

ABOUT THE AUTHOR

L ana Shabdeen was born in Uzbekistan and came to California with her whole family when she was 16. Always into self-help and personal growth, she hopes this book will inspire you to grow as an individual, to be happy, and to love yourself, no matter what. She still lives in California with her husband, Rim, two beautiful daughters, Amelia and Ariana, and a Maltipoo dog named Jake.

Printed in Great Britain
by Amazon

45151594R00116